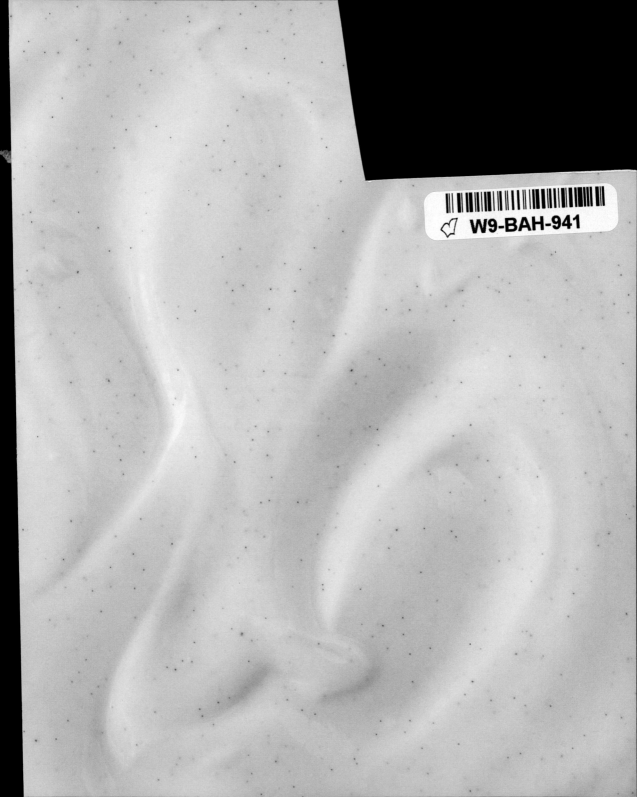

Chefs

Host

A COOK'S GUIDE TO BLITZING THE HOLIDAY SEASON

Christmas

Too.

Hardie Grant

BOOKS

Sides
(± salads).
42–61

Remains
of the day.
158–169

Introduction.

Hold on to your Santa hats, Christmas is here! You've been counting down the days and you've bought all the pressies, and this year it's your turn to host. All the relatives have already confirmed they're coming. There's no need to panic...

But...what are you going to cook?

Oh, the stress and worry of it all. Does Uncle Quinn even like seafood? Don't forget Hannah is now a vegetarian. Is cousin Emma's new boyfriend coming? Will he eat anything, or is he a fussy so and so, too? Should you make it a traditional or non-traditional lunch? What to do! Are you gonna do roast spuds? Have you even ordered the ham yet? And why bother with the brussels sprouts? No one eats them. Arrrgh! It's too hard.

Wait! Stop. Pour yourself a mulled wine and let me help. This book has the lot...and so much more. Take a flick through and find my suggestions for some nibbles to go with that much-needed drink. There's advice on alternatives to a boring roast turkey and I'll tell you the secret to the crispiest roast potatoes. Want a showstopping main? It's all in here. Do you need help on dessert? I know a thing or two about that as well.

Think of this book as a little survival guide to the holiday season – it has everything you need to totally crush Christmas. Everyone will be thanking you and trying to invite themselves back next year. They'll be raving about your salads, impressed by your thoughtful edible gifts, and that Christmas trifle will be the talk of the town. Seriously, you are going to look like an absolute superstar! When Christmas is mentioned in years to come, 'Careless Whisper' by George Michael will spring to mind, closely followed by your magnificent pavlova.

It's the best time of year – I love it, so I wrote a book.
Now, Christmas is yours...own it.

Merry Christmas!

ORANGE + SOY-
GLAZED WHOLE
ROASTED DUCK

p72

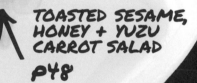

TOASTED SESAME,
HONEY + YUZU
CARROT SALAD
p48

Sample menus.

The traditional

Start

Oysters mignonette	**p 29**
Grilled prawn cocktail	**p 33**

Main

Turkey saltimbocca	**p 64**
Cranberry, walnut + whisky sauce	**p 4**
Cheesy polenta w sweet corn	**p 44**
Brussels sprouts slaw	**p 45**
Pork, leek, sage + fennel stuffing	**p 59**

Dessert + cheese

The Christmas pudding	**p 114**
Garlic + rosemary–baked Vacherin Mont d'Or	**p 128**
Mince pies	**p 92**
Chocolate-infused rum + dark chocolate truffles	**p 152**

The luxe

Start

Sashimi tartare	**p 28**
Oysters w Champagne + finger lime	**p 31**
Scotch quail eggs	**p 40**
Seafood platter	**p 77**

Main

Beef wellington	**p 67**
Duck-fat roasted potatoes	**p 60**
Fried brussels sprouts w white anchovy, walnut garlic + pecorino	**p 46**
Cauliflower cheese	**p 58**

Dessert + cheese

Christmas trifle	**p 99**
The cheeseboard	**p 130**
Salted caramels	**p 154**

A seafood surprise

The celebration

This book uses 15 ml (½ fl oz) tablespoons; cooks with 20 ml (¾ fl oz) tablespoons should be scant with their tablespoon measurements.

It also uses metric cup measurements, i.e. 250 ml for 1 cup; in the US a cup is 8 fl oz, just smaller, and American cooks should be generous in their cup measurements; in the UK a cup is 10 fl oz and British cooks should be scant with their cup measurements.

Equipment.

The recipes in this book aren't hard for you to make at home – and you certainly don't need any fancy kitchen gear. You know, the stuff you rushed out to buy after you watched that cooking show. There is no reason for you to buy a Dewar flask and start googling liquid nitrogen supplier companies. You will need a few bits though. I guess they aren't essential, but you will get better and more consistent results if you invest in the following pieces of equipment.

Digital scales
Leave the guesswork to a Christmas Day game of charades. To make (and nail) these dishes you need to follow the recipe. That means weighing out ingredients correctly; and that means a good set of digital scales.

Knives
You'll need different knives for different jobs. It is well worth investing in and maintaining a set of knives. Carving, chopping, slicing and small paring jobs all need a different knife. Keep them sharp and your food will always look professionally done.

Piping (icing) bags
Disposable or not, these are great to direct creams and mixes onto cakes and desserts.

Digital thermometer
So handy for so many things: making marshmallow, melting chocolate and testing the 'doneness' of meat. This is a must-have in my kitchen; I absolutely could not live without one. They are relatively inexpensive as well – and what's $15 when you have probably spent twice that on assembling a beef wellington. You don't want to overcook the beef; that would be a shame. So, be good and ask Santa for a digital thermometer.

Microwave oven
This is perfect for melting small quantities of chocolate. Think of Chef Mike as your own little sous chef.

Blow torch
Not strictly essential but they are useful for lightly toasting meringue or marshmallow, or for crisping up that piece of pork crackling.

Chef's little helpers.

(THINGS YOU'LL WANT)

Cocktail sauce.

Makes 450 g (1 lb)

3 egg yolks
1 tablespoon lemon juice
2 tablespoons warm water
pinch of salt flakes
250 ml (8½ fl oz/1 cup) light
    olive oil
2 tablespoons tomato sauce
    (ketchup)
2 teaspoons worcestershire
    sauce
2 teaspoons sriracha sauce
    or hot chilli sauce
1 teaspoon grated fresh
    horseradish or store-bought
    horseradish cream
½ teaspoon cayenne pepper
1 tablespoon brandy

1/ Combine the egg yolks, lemon juice, warm water and salt in a tall, narrow measuring jug. Process well using a hand-held blender.

2/ Continue to blend while you add a tablespoon of oil to the jug. Mix until it emulsifies, then slowly trickle in the remaining oil. Continue to blend in an up and down motion until you have mayonnaise. Add the remaining ingredients and blend well.

3/ Cover and store in the fridge for up to 3 days. Serve with the Grilled prawn cocktail (page 33) and as an accompaniment to the Seafood platter (page 77).

Apple sauce.

Makes 250 g (9 oz)

30 g (1 oz) butter
3 granny smith apples, or other
    tart cooking apples, peeled
    and chopped into 5 mm
    (¼ in) dice
2 tablespoons caster (superfine)
    sugar
1 teaspoon apple cider vinegar
finely grated zest of 1 lemon

1/ Melt the butter in a saucepan over medium heat and add the apples. Stir and cook for 8 minutes. Add the sugar and cook for a further 4–5 minutes.

2/ Remove from the heat and stir in the vinegar and lemon zest. Cool and serve with the Pork rack w crispy crackling (page 80).

Chilli mayonnaise.

Makes 350 g (12½ oz)

3 egg yolks
1 tablespoon lemon juice
2 tablespoons warm water
pinch of salt flakes
250 ml (8½ fl oz/1 cup) light olive oil
chilli sauce, to taste

1/ Combine the egg yolks, lemon juice, warm water and salt in a tall, narrow measuring jug. Process well using a hand-held blender.

2/ Continue to blend while you add a tablespoon of oil to the jug. Mix until it emulsifies, then slowly trickle in the remaining oil. Continue to blend in an up and down motion until you have mayonnaise. Blend in the chilli sauce. Cover and store in the fridge for up to 3 days. Serve with Scotch quail eggs (page 40).

Horseradish crème fraîche.

Makes 350 g (12½ oz)

250 g (9 oz) crème fraîche, at room temperature
2 tablespoons grated fresh horseradish or store-bought horseradish cream
juice of ½ lemon
pinch of salt flakes

1/ Using a spoon, mix all the ingredients together in a bowl. Store in the fridge for up to 3 days. Serve with Gin-cured ocean trout (page 37).

Quick pickled cucumbers.

Makes 250 g (9 oz)

1 French shallot
80 ml (2½ fl oz/⅓ cup) white wine vinegar
2 teaspoons caster (superfine) sugar
1 teaspoon salt flakes
1 Lebanese (long) cucumber
1 tablespoon fresh dill fronds

1/ Peel the shallot and thinly slice using a mandoline or sharp knife. Separate the slices and soak them in a bowl of boiling water. Leave for 10 minutes then drain.

2/ Combine the vinegar, sugar and salt in a small saucepan over medium heat, stirring to dissolve the sugar. Remove from the heat and set aside to cool.

3/ Cut the cucumber on the diagonal into 2 mm (⅛ in) thick slices and place in a bowl. Pour the cooled vinegar mixture over the cucumber. Add the shallot rings and dill and then set aside for 20 minutes before serving. Serve with the Gin-cured ocean trout (page 37) and with Cucumber, zucchini ± fennel w goat's curd ± dill (page 49).

Cranberry, walnut ± whisky sauce.

Makes 4 x 300 g (10½ oz) jars

185 ml (6 fl oz/¾ cup) water
160 g (5½ oz) caster (superfine)
    sugar
500 g (1 lb 2 oz) fresh
    cranberries
100 g (3½ oz) dried cranberries,
    chopped
100 g (3½ oz/1 cup) walnut
    halves, toasted and chopped
finely grated zest and juice of
    2 oranges
100 ml (3½ fl oz) whisky

Chef's note
Make this using frozen (thawed)
cranberries instead of fresh
ones if living in Oz, as fresh
cranberries are hard to come
by. In the US the cranberry
harvest is during autumn (fall),
and this is the perfect time
to make this sauce.

1/ Put the water and sugar in a saucepan over medium heat and stir to dissolve the sugar. Bring to the boil and add the fresh cranberries, then continue to cook for about 5 minutes, or until most of the cranberries have expanded and burst open.

2/ Remove from the heat and add the dried cranberries and walnuts followed by the orange zest and juice. Mix well, then stir in the whisky.

3/ Transfer the sauce into plastic containers and store in the fridge. Alternatively, pour into sterilised jars and store in the pantry for up to 6 months. Refrigerate after opening and use within 1 month. This is a handy sauce to have in the fridge, not only at Christmas for your turkey (see page 64) but throughout the year – as an accompaniment to other roasted meats (either hot or cold), or even cheese, and it is particularly great in cold meat sandwiches.

Gravy.

Makes 300 ml (10¼ fl oz)

60 ml (2 oz/¼ cup) light
   olive oil
3 French shallots, sliced
salt flakes
1 carrot, peeled and sliced
2 celery stalks, trimmed
   and sliced
3 garlic cloves, peeled
   and smashed
1 tablespoon fresh thyme leaves
1 bay leaf
200 ml (7 fl oz) white wine

600 ml (20 fl oz) chicken stock
2 tablespoons plain
   (all-purpose) flour
1 tablespoon worcestershire
   sauce
1 tablespoon chardonnay
   vinegar
freshly ground black pepper
1 tablespoon chopped fresh
   tarragon
1 teaspoon chopped fresh sage
50 g (1¾ oz) unsalted butter

1/ Heat the oil in a saucepan over medium–high heat and add the shallots and ½ teaspoon salt. Fry the shallots for 2 minutes, stirring regularly, then add the carrot, celery and garlic. Fry for a few minutes until the vegetables are soft, then add the thyme and bay leaf and cook for a further 2 minutes.

2/ Deglaze the pan with the wine, making sure you scrape any 'caught' bits on the base of the pan into the sauce. Cook until the wine has reduced by half, then add 200 ml (7 fl oz) of the stock and again cook to reduce the liquid in the pan. Once most of the liquid has reduced, reduce the heat to medium and add the flour, stirring it in well to coat the vegetables.

3/ Add the remaining stock, the worcestershire sauce and vinegar. Reduce the heat to low and simmer for 30 minutes, stirring occasionally. Season with salt and pepper to taste.

4/ Turn off the heat and stir in the chopped tarragon and sage. Leave to infuse for 30 minutes, then strain the gravy through a sieve into a small saucepan so it's ready for reheating. Discard the vegetables.

5/ To serve, reheat the gravy and whisk in the butter until melted. Check the seasoning and pour into a gravy jug.

Custard/brandy custard.

<u>Makes</u> 800 g (1 lb 12 oz)

275 ml (9½ fl oz) thickened
   (whipping) cream
275 ml (9½ fl oz) full-cream
   (whole) milk
1 vanilla bean, seeds scraped
95 g (3¼ oz) caster (superfine)
   sugar
20 g (¾ oz) cornflour
   (cornstarch)
3 egg yolks
75 ml (2½ fl oz) brandy
   (optional)

1/ Combine the cream, milk, vanilla bean and seeds in a saucepan over low–medium heat. Bring to a simmer, then remove the pan from the heat and discard the vanilla bean.

2/ Put the sugar, cornflour and egg yolks in a bowl and whisk together until the mixture pales and thickens.

3/ Pour one-third of the hot cream mixture onto the egg yolk mixture in the bowl and whisk well to combine. Pour this back into the pan with the remaining cream mixture and mix well with a spatula or wooden spoon.

4/ Return the pan to low–medium heat and whisk constantly until the custard starts to boil and bubble. Cook at this temperature for a further 20 seconds, stirring constantly, then stir in the brandy if using. Serve while warm.

5/ Alternatively, transfer the warm custard to the bowl of a freestanding electric mixer fitted with the paddle attachment. Mix the custard on low to medium speed until it cools to room temperature – this will prevent your custard getting lumpy as it cools. Cover and store in the fridge until needed. This is the perfect sauce to serve with your triumphant Christmas pudding (page 114).

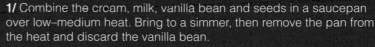

Champagne sabayon.

<u>Makes</u> 500 g (1 lb 2 oz)

180 ml (6 fl oz/¾ cup) thickened
   (whipping) cream
150 ml (5 fl oz) Champagne
   or sparkling wine
5 egg yolks
70 g (2½ oz) caster (superfine)
   sugar

1/ Whisk the cream in a bowl until you have a thick ribbon. Refrigerate until needed.

2/ Put the Champagne, egg yolks and sugar in a large metal bowl. Place the bowl over a saucepan of gently simmering water, ensuring the base of the bowl isn't touching the water. Whisk by hand for 3–4 minutes until the mixture becomes thick and pale.

3/ Remove the bowl from the heat and whisk by hand for a further minute. Chill the bowl in the fridge for 5 minutes and then gently fold in the cream. Transfer to a serving bowl and serve within an hour. Use this for a layer in the Christmas trifle (page 99), to serve with the Fruit salad <u>w</u> peach schnapps (page 126) and with the Moscato ± raspberry jelly (page 105).

Hot chocolate sauce.

Makes 500 ml (17 fl oz/2 cups)

150 ml (5 fl oz) thickened
  (whipping) cream
150 ml (5 fl oz) full-cream
  (whole) milk
40 g (1½ oz) caster (superfine)
  sugar
200 g (7 oz) chopped dark
  chocolate, or chocolate melts
  (buttons)

1/ Put the cream, milk and sugar in a saucepan over medium heat and bring to the boil. Remove from the heat and stir in the chocolate. Stir until the sauce is smooth and serve immediately. Serve this over ice cream or with the Hot banana, rum ± raisin caramel puddings (page 95).

Vanilla sauce.

Makes 650 ml (22 fl oz)

250 ml (8½ fl oz/1 cup)
  full-cream (whole) milk
200 ml (7 fl oz) thickened
  (whipping) cream
2 vanilla beans, seeds scraped
5 egg yolks
100 g (3½ oz) caster (superfine)
  sugar

1/ Prepare a large bowl of ice and place a medium-sized bowl on top – this is to cool down the custard base once cooked.

2/ Put the milk, cream, vanilla seeds, egg yolks and sugar in a bowl and whisk to combine. Pour the mixture into a heavy-based saucepan over low heat and add the vanilla bean. Stir continuously with a spatula or spoon and cook to 82°C (180°F); use a digital thermometer to accurately check the temperature.

3/ Remove the pan from the heat and strain the custard through a sieve into the bowl on the ice.

4/ Stir the custard until it cools to 50°C (122°F) and then transfer the mix into the fridge to finish cooling for a minimum of 4 hours.

5/ This sauce is best made the day before you need to use it, to give it time to cool and thicken naturally. Make a batch of this and you can make all sorts of stuff. Like what? Well, the Muscat ± raisin ice cream sandwiches (page 120) for a start, or the Eggnog (page 13), and a luxury sauce for desserts such as the Gingerbread-spiced pumpkin pie (page 106).

White chocolate ± vanilla cream.

Makes about 1 kg (2 lb 3 oz)

360 g (12½ oz) white chocolate,
   melted (see page 98)
2 vanilla beans, seeds scraped
720 ml (24½ fl oz) thickened
   (whipping) cream

1/ Put the melted chocolate and vanilla seeds in a heatproof bowl. Heat 250 ml (8½ fl oz/1 cup) of the cream in a saucepan until it just reaches boiling point, then pour onto the melted chocolate. Leave for 30 seconds before stirring with a spatula to combine well.

2/ Stir in the remaining cold cream. Pour the cream mixture into a container, cover and chill in the fridge for 2 hours or so.

3/ Transfer the cream to the bowl of a freestanding electric mixer fitted with the whisk attachment. Whisk the cream on medium speed to firm peaks. This cream can be used for the Christmas trifle (page 99) and is also great for tarts and served with fresh fruit.

Whipped brandy orange butter.

Makes 340 g (12 oz)

250 g (9 oz) unsalted cultured
   butter, softened
pinch of salt
40 g (1½ oz/⅓ cup) icing
   (confectioners') sugar
finely grated zest of ½ orange
50 ml (1¾ fl oz) brandy or
   cognac

1/ Whip the butter until pale using a freestanding electric mixer or electric beaters. Add the salt, icing sugar and orange zest and beat again for a couple of minutes. Continue to beat as you trickle in the brandy. Store in the fridge for up to 1 week. Lather this all over those warm Mince pies (page 92).

Apple compote.

Makes 600 g (1 lb 5 oz)

100 g (3½ oz) caster (superfine)
    sugar
300 ml (10 fl oz) apple juice
1 vanilla bean, seeds scraped
3 granny smith apples, or
    other tart cooking apples,
    peeled and chopped into
    5 mm (¼ in) dice

1/ Put the sugar in a saucepan with the apple juice and vanilla seeds. Bring to the boil over medium heat and cook for 2 minutes, stirring constantly.

2/ Add the apples and cook until they begin to soften, stirring regularly. Remove from the heat and leave to cool. Apple compote is great to have on hand to make pies and crumbles, and is used in the filling for Mince pies (page 92).

HIC*

Drinks.

(BOOZE MOSTLY)

Mulled wine.

This is my take on mulled wine – the warm and fuzzy drink popular in the northern hemisphere at Christmas. There's nothing better than lighting the fire, popping on a Christmas movie and warming yourself up with a mulled wine (or two). The awesome thing about this drink is its versatility: try it with white wine instead of red if you like, experiment with your own combination of spices and herbs, or sweeten it further by adding a touch of honey. On hot days it can even be served cold over ice.

Chef's note
For a non-alcoholic version, replace the red wine and pedro ximénez with a good-quality apple or pear juice.

Serves 12

150 g (5½ oz/⅔ cup) caster (superfine) sugar
250 ml (8½ fl oz/1 cup) apple juice (organic fresh pressed or juiced)
2 x 750 ml (25½ fl oz) bottles pinot noir
375 ml (12½ fl oz/1½ cups) pedro ximénez or sweet sherry

2 oranges, zest cut into strips, pith removed
1 lemon, zest cut into strips, pith removed
15 cloves
10 star anise
5 cinnamon sticks
½ teaspoon freshly grated nutmeg
2 vanilla beans, seeds scraped
10 g (¼ oz) ginger, peeled and sliced

1/ Place a large cast-iron pot on the stovetop over medium heat. Once hot, add the sugar and reduce the heat to low. Stir the sugar with a spatula or spoon for 5–7 minutes, until the sugar has melted and turned a deep amber caramel.

2/ Add the apple juice slowly, stirring constantly. Be careful of spitting and **hot** steam, as the mixture will expand and bubble initially before settling down.

3/ Once all the apple juice has been added, add the remaining ingredients, including the scraped vanilla beans, and bring up to a temperature of 80°C (176°F); use a digital thermometer to check the temperature. Cover with a lid, turn off the heat and leave to infuse for a minimum of 1 hour.

4/ When you are ready to serve, take the lid off and reheat on the stove. Ladle into heatproof glasses.

Cherry bellini.

Serves 4

8 Cherries in vanilla syrup
    (page 134)
1 x 750 ml (25½ fl oz) bottle
    prosecco
4 tablespoons peach nectar

1/ Take four champagne flutes and place two drained cherries into each glass.

2/ Open the prosecco and carefully pour it onto the cherries in the glass. If you pour the prosecco slowly and steadily into the centre of each glass, you should be able to fill the glass without it going over. Leave a 2 cm (¾ in) gap at the top of each glass.

3/ Slowly pour in the peach nectar over the back of a teaspoon. Serve immediately.

Eggnog.

Serves 6

375 ml (12½ oz/1½ cups) Vanilla
    sauce (page 7)
160 ml (5½ fl oz) spiced rum,
    brandy or bourbon
80 ml (2½ fl oz/⅓ cup) full-
    cream (whole) milk
80 ml (2½ fl oz/⅓ cup)
    thickened (whipping) cream
8 ice cubes
freshly grated nutmeg,
    to garnish

1/ Pour the vanilla sauce, alcohol, milk and cream into a cocktail shaker with the ice cubes and seal the top with a pint glass. Shake like a cocktail for 1 minute.

2/ Strain the drink into six glasses and grate a little nutmeg over the top. Serve immediately.

EGGNOG p13

MULLED WINE
p12

ESPRESSO MARTINI
p16

CHERRY BELLINI p13

Pineapple rum punch.

Serves 10

50 g (1¾ oz) caster (superfine)
    sugar
50 ml (1¾ fl oz) water
1 kg (2 lb 3 oz) pineapple flesh
500 ml (17 fl oz/2 cups) spiced
    rum
75 ml (2½ fl oz) malibu
crushed ice

1/ Boil the sugar and water in a saucepan over low heat, stirring constantly until the sugar dissolves. Bring to the boil, then remove the pan from the heat and allow the syrup to cool.

2/ Blitz the sugar syrup and pineapple flesh in a blender for a few minutes until super smooth. Strain the juice into a bowl and add the rum and malibu. Fill tall glasses with crushed ice and top with the punch.

Watermelon ± strawberry frosé.

Serves 12

1 kg (2 lb 3 oz) watermelon flesh
500 g (1 lb 2 oz) strawberries,
    hulled
1 x 750 ml (25½ fl oz) bottle
    rosé wine
100 ml (3½ fl oz) peach
    schnapps

1/ Blitz the watermelon and strawberries in a blender for a few minutes until super smooth. Strain the juice into a bowl and add the wine and schnapps.

2/ Transfer the mix into shallow plastic containers and freeze overnight. Use a blender to blitz the frozen cubes. Pour into chilled glasses and serve.

Espresso martini.

Serves 10

ice cubes
100 ml (3½ fl oz) milk
80 ml (2½ fl oz/⅓ cup) espresso,
    freshly made
50 ml (1¾ fl oz) sugar syrup (see
    step 1, Pineapple rum punch)

Coffee-infused vodka
150 g (5½ oz) coffee beans,
    coarsely crushed
1 x 700 ml (23½ fl oz) bottle
    vodka

1/ For the coffee-infused vodka, combine the crushed coffee beans and vodka in a bowl, then cover and leave in the pantry for 1 week to allow the flavours to develop. Strain the vodka through muslin (cheesecloth), discarding the coffee beans. Reserve 250 ml (8½ fl oz/1 cup) for this recipe and store the remaining infused vodka in the original bottle in the freezer.

2/ Chill some martini glasses in the freezer. Fill a cocktail shaker with ice cubes and add the coffee-infused vodka, milk, espresso and sugar syrup. Stir for 2 minutes and then strain into the glasses.

PINEAPPLE RUM PUNCH
p16

Snacks ± starters.

(NIBBLY THINGS)

Christmas nibbles.

There is a lot going on at Christmas – lots of people, guests dropping in…lots of drinks – so you're gonna need a few bits and pieces on hand for everyone to munch on while they catch up. I remember my own childhood Christmases where Mum used to put salted nuts, whole nuts (with a nut cracker), cheese straws and other nibbles around the house to keep us all going. Serve a few of these recipes to your guests and they might stay a bit longer or visit more regularly. Of course, if that thought terrifies you, then leave these well alone.

Cheese straws.

Makes 30

375 g (13 oz) puff pastry sheet
    (I make my own or use
    Carême brand)
4 egg yolks
1 tablespoon milk
100 g (3½ oz/1 cup) finely grated
    parmesan cheese
2 teaspoons smoked paprika

1/ Lightly flour the work surface and use a rolling pin to roll the puff pastry to a 3 mm (⅛ in) thick rectangle. Cut into two equal halves.

2/ Combine the egg yolks and milk, then brush the egg wash over the top of one piece of pastry. Mix the parmesan with the paprika and sprinkle one-third of the cheese mix evenly onto the egg wash, ensuring the surface of the pastry is covered. Lay the second piece of pastry directly on top of the cheese surface.

3/ Use a rolling pin to press the top pastry sheet down so it sticks to the bottom sheet. Brush the top with egg wash and sprinkle half of the remaining cheese mix on top, again ensuring the surface is evenly covered. Push the cheese down with your hands to stick.

4/ Lightly flour the work surface and flip the sheets of puff pastry over so the cheese is now on the bottom. Brush the last exposed surface of pastry with egg wash and cover with the remaining cheese. Press down.

5/ Working from one of the longest sides, roll the pastry up to form a scroll. Cover in plastic wrap and refrigerate for 30 minutes.

6/ Preheat the oven to 180°C (350°F). Line a large baking tray with baking paper.

7/ Use a knife to cut the pastry scroll into 1 cm (½ in) thick slices. Working with one slice at a time, open it out a little at first and then all of the way while twisting the slice into a long straw shape. Roll the straw with your hands until it is the length of the baking tray. Place on the tray and repeat, spacing the straws 2 cm (¾ in) apart.

8/ When the tray is full, transfer it to the oven and bake the straws for 16 minutes, or until golden brown and crisp. Remove from the oven and leave to cool on the tray before serving.

Olive oil croutons.

Makes 60

1 small baguette or ficelle
olive oil for brushing
3–4 garlic cloves, cut in half
salt flakes

Chef's note
A ficelle, or *pain ficelle*, is a
French bread loaf similar to
a baguette but thinner.

1/ Cut the baguette into three pieces and place into the freezer for
30 minutes to semi-freeze. Preheat the oven to 160°C (320°F). Line
a baking tray with baking paper.

2/ Thinly slice the bread using a sharp knife and place the slices
on the tray. Brush each one with oil, place a sheet of baking paper
over the top, then put another tray on top and gently push down to
flatten the slices a little.

3/ Bake for 12–14 minutes, or until the croutons are golden brown.
Remove from the oven, lift off the top tray and remove the paper.
Rub each slice with the cut garlic and sprinkle salt flakes over
the top. Serve with the dips in this chapter (pages 23–4) and with
Sashimi tartare (page 28).

Parmesan grissini.

Makes 40

225 g (8 oz/1½ cups) wholemeal
   (whole-wheat) flour
225 g (8 oz/1½ cups) plain
   (all-purpose) flour, plus extra
   for dusting
70 g (2½ oz/¾ cup) finely grated
   parmesan
1 teaspoon salt
7 g (¼ oz) active dried yeast
2 tablespoons olive oil
220 ml (7½ fl oz) cold tap water
canola oil spray

1/ Place all the ingredients in the bowl of a freestanding electric
mixer fitted with the dough hook. Knead for 8 minutes on medium
speed until you have a smooth and elastic dough. Remove from
the machine and lay a damp tea towel over the bowl. Leave at
room temperature for 30 minutes.

2/ Preheat the oven to 180°C (350°F). Line a baking tray with
baking paper. Remove the tea towel from the bowl. Lightly flour
the work surface and knock the dough back onto it by slamming
it down. Using a rolling pin, roll out the dough to a 5 mm (¼ in)
thickness, regularly lifting the dough and lightly flouring the work
surface as you go, to ensure the dough doesn't stick.

3/ Use a knife to cut the dough into strips about 1 cm (½ in) thick.
Place the strips on the tray and then put the tray in the warmest
area of your kitchen. Lightly spray the sticks with oil spray and
lay a sheet of plastic wrap over the top to cover. Leave the dough
strips to prove for 20 minutes.

4/ Lightly dust the strips with flour, then bake for 10–12 minutes
until golden and crisp. Transfer to a wire rack to cool. Store the
grissini in an airtight container for up to 2 days, or freeze for up
to 1 month for later use (reheat in a 180°C/350°F oven).

Savoury thins or lavosh.

Makes 20–30 savoury thins
or 15–20 lavosh

480 g (1 lb 1 oz/3¼ cups)
    strong (baker's) flour
150 ml (5 fl oz) olive oil, plus
    extra for brushing
220 ml (7½ fl oz) cold tap water
3 teaspoons garlic salt
canola oil spray
sesame seeds for garnish
    (for the savoury thins)
salt flakes for garnish
    (for the lavosh)

1/ Put the flour, olive oil, water and garlic salt in the bowl of a freestanding electric mixer fitted with the dough hook. Knead for 15–20 minutes on low to medium speed until you have a smooth and elastic dough.

2/ Turn the dough out onto a lightly floured work surface and spray the dough with a little oil spray. Cover with plastic wrap and rest for 30 minutes.

3/ Preheat the oven to 165°C (330°F). Lightly spray a flat baking tray or baking sheet with a little oil spray, line with baking paper and use your hands to smooth the paper out flat.

4/ For the savoury thins, divide the dough into four equal pieces. Using a rolling pin, roll out one piece of dough on a lightly floured work surface. Once it is half the size of the tray, transfer it to the prepared tray. Use your fingertips to gently pull the dough to stretch it outwards and lengthways to fit the size of the tray. Try to get the sheets super thin, but take care not to tear any holes (no stress if you do).

5/ Brush the dough with a little extra olive oil and sprinkle sesame seeds on top. Bake for 6–8 minutes until light golden and cooked. Remove from the oven and allow to cool before breaking into irregular pieces. Repeat these steps with the remaining three pieces of dough.

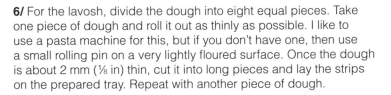

6/ For the lavosh, divide the dough into eight equal pieces. Take one piece of dough and roll it out as thinly as possible. I like to use a pasta machine for this, but if you don't have one, then use a small rolling pin on a very lightly floured surface. Once the dough is about 2 mm (⅛ in) thin, cut it into long pieces and lay the strips on the prepared tray. Repeat with another piece of dough.

7/ Brush the dough with olive oil and sprinkle with salt. Bake for 6–8 minutes until light golden. Repeat these steps with the remaining six pieces of dough.

Christmas dips.

Christmas is all about feeding people in between feeding people, and to do that you need to be able to satisfy a crowd quickly so you can crack on with everything else. Dips are super easy to make, keep the hunger pangs at bay, and are so much better in taste and nutrition than store bought. You can use some of the nibbles on pages 20–2 for dipping, or even raw vegetables such as capsicums (peppers), carrots and celery.

Avocado, coriander ± lime dip.

<u>Makes</u> 600 g (1 lb 5 oz)

3 ripe avocados
1 garlic clove, grated with a microplane
finely grated zest and juice of 2 limes
2 tablespoons chopped fresh coriander (cilantro) leaves
1 red bird's eye chilli, seeded and chopped
salt flakes, to taste
freshly ground black pepper, to taste

1/ Cut the avocados in half and remove the stones, then use a spoon to scoop the flesh into a blender. Add the remaining ingredients and blend until smooth. Taste and adjust the seasoning if necessary.

2/ Alternatively, for a coarser consistency, put all the ingredients in a bowl and use a fork to mash everything together.

3/ Transfer the dip to a bowl and serve immediately.

Yoghurt dip.

<u>Makes</u> 650 g (1 lb 7 oz)

500 g (1 lb 2 oz/2 cups) Greek-style yoghurt
1 garlic clove, grated with a microplane
finely grated zest and juice of 1 lemon
1 tablespoon chopped fresh flat-leaf (Italian) parsley
1 tablespoon chopped fresh mint
1 tablespoon chopped fresh dill
salt flakes
freshly ground black pepper
2 tablespoons cumin seeds, toasted and ground
75 ml (2½ fl oz) light olive oil

1/ Mix the yoghurt with the garlic, lemon zest, juice and herbs. Season with salt and pepper to taste.

2/ Transfer to a serving bowl, sprinkle the cumin over the top and drizzle with the oil. Give one stir with a spoon to gently combine, and serve.

Whipped cod roe.

Makes 850 g (1 lb 14 oz)

150 g (5½ oz) white bread
500 ml (17 fl oz/2 cups) warm
*   water*
150 g (5½ oz) salted cod roe
juice of 1 lemon
2 French shallots, finely diced
1 garlic clove, peeled
400 ml (13½ fl oz) light olive oil
freshly ground black pepper

Market
Buy salted cod roe from your
local deli or fishmonger.

1/ Cut the bread into 5 cm (2 in) dice and put them in a bowl.
Pour the warm water over the bread and set aside to soak for
5 minutes until soft.

2/ Gently squeeze the excess water out of the bread. Put the bread
in a blender with the cod roe, lemon juice and shallots. Finely
grate in the garlic using a microplane. Blend on high speed until
combined, then, with the motor running, slowly add the oil until the
mixture is smooth.

3/ Season to taste with pepper and serve, or cover and refrigerate
until needed.

Roast carrot, capsicum, chilli ± coriander dip.

Makes 1.2 kg (2 lb 10 oz)

1 kg (2 lb 3 oz) carrots, peeled
*   and cut into equal-sized pieces*
2 red capsicums (peppers),
*   seeded and flesh chopped into*
*   large equal-sized pieces*
1 large green chilli, cut in half
*   (seeds left in)*
2 garlic cloves, peeled
150 ml (5 fl oz) light olive oil
1 tablespoon coriander seeds
salt flakes to taste
finely grated zest and juice of
*   1 lemon*
warm water as needed
150 g (5½ oz) Greek-style yoghurt
1 red bird's eye chilli, chopped
*   with seeds*
4 tablespoons thinly sliced fresh
*   coriander (cilantro) leaves*

1/ Preheat the oven to 180°C (350°F). Put the carrot, capsicum,
green chilli and garlic cloves on a large baking tray and drizzle
with half the oil. Add the coriander seeds and salt and shake the
tray to coat the vegetables. Place the tray in the oven and cook
for 1 hour, or until the vegetables are nicely roasted.

2/ Transfer the contents of the tray into a blender. Blend on high
speed for a few minutes, then add the lemon zest and lemon juice
and drizzle in the remaining oil. Adjust the consistency by adding
warm water, a little at a time.

3/ Transfer the dip into a bowl and stir in the yoghurt, chilli and
coriander. Cover and refrigerate for a few hours before serving.

WHIPPED
COD ROE
p24

ROAST CARROT, CAPSICUM,
CHILLI + CORIANDER DIP
p24

p23
AVOCADO, CORIANDER
+ LIME DIP

SASHIMI TARTARE
p28

CHEESE STRAWS
p20

OYSTERS BAKED
W HORSERADISH
+ PARMESAN
p29

Sashimi tartare.

This awesome starter or snack is filled with flavour and freshness, and is something you can whip up in minutes. Serve this on individual plates as a starter, or in a large bowl with a pile of Olive oil croutons (page 21) for nibbles.

Market
When serving raw fish it's important that you buy fish that is sashimi grade. Pre-order your fish from the market or your fishmonger to avoid disappointment at Christmas. If you don't fancy salmon, then substitute with sashimi-grade tuna or kingfish.

Serves
6 as a starter; more if sharing as nibbles

Prep time
15 minutes

Cook time
Nil

600 g (1 lb 5 oz) sashimi-grade salmon, cut into 5 mm (¼ in) dice
150 g (5½ oz) assorted cherry tomatoes, cut into 5 mm (¼ in) dice
1 avocado, cut into 5 mm (¼ in) dice
1 red bird's eye chilli, seeded and finely chopped
finely grated zest and juice of 2 limes
2 tablespoons thinly sliced fresh coriander (cilantro) leaves
2 tablespoons tamari sauce

1/ Put all the ingredients in a bowl and gently stir to combine. Serve immediately.

Oysters.

When you think 'celebration', you think 'oysters and Champagne'. If Christmas is the ultimate celebration of family and friends, then these two things simply MUST be on the menu. There are many ways to serve oysters, but here are a couple of suggestions that just happen to be my favourite ways to enjoy them. Bust these out to set the tone for an epic celebration!

Oysters mignonette.

Makes 24

2 dozen unopened fresh oysters
150 ml (5 fl oz) cabernet merlot vinegar
4 French shallots, diced ultra finely
freshly ground white pepper

1/ Open the oysters (see page 32) and arrange them in a dish on a bed of crushed ice.

2/ For the mignonette sauce, combine the vinegar, shallots and a little white pepper in a small serving bowl. Serve the sauce separately so your guests can dress the oysters themselves.

Oysters baked <u>w</u> horseradish ± parmesan.

Makes 24

2 dozen unopened fresh oysters
125 g (4½ oz) unsalted butter, softened
200 g (7 oz) parmesan, finely grated with a microplane
100 g (3½ oz) horseradish cream
2 teaspoons worcestershire sauce
2 tablespoons chopped fresh flat-leaf (Italian) parsley
finely grated zest of 1 lemon
freshly ground black pepper, to taste
thin lemon wedges, to serve

1/ Open the oysters (see page 32) and place them on a baking tray. Preheat the grill (broiler) to high. Arrange the oven shelf so it is sitting just below the grill.

2/ Put all the remaining ingredients (except the lemon wedges) in a bowl and mix with a spoon to combine well. Spread ½ tablespoon of the mix onto each oyster, then divide any remaining mixture evenly among the oysters.

3/ Place the tray in the oven and grill (broil) for 4 minutes to melt the cheese mixture and finish the oysters. Remove and serve immediately, with some lemon wedges for squeezing over.

Oysters w̲ Champagne ± finger lime.

Makes̲ 24

375 ml (12½ fl oz/1½ cups)
  Champagne or sparkling wine
2 dozen unopened fresh oysters
6 fresh finger limes

1/ Pour the Champagne into a plastic container and freeze for a minimum of 5 hours, or until frozen hard. Use a fork to scrape the Champagne granita into fine crystals. Return to the freezer.

2/ Open the oysters (see page 32) and arrange them in a dish on a bed of crushed ice.

3/ Cut the limes in half lengthways and spoon some of the citrusy 'caviar' onto each oyster. Top with some Champagne granita and serve immediately.

On oysters.

Buying
If you can, buy your oysters unshucked (in unopened shells) or order them in advance from your fishmonger. To ensure you're getting the best and freshest, choose local and what's in season. Buy your oysters as close as possible to serving day, to minimise storage times.

If you do buy shucked oysters, ask when they were opened. If it was that day, then buy them, but you need to eat them on the day.

Storing
Wrap unshucked oysters in a damp tea towel or cloth and put them in the bottom of the fridge. In cooler climates you can leave them out of the fridge, wrapped in a tea towel – 12°C–14°C (54°F–57°F) is an ideal temperature in the pantry – but here in Oz, your kitchen at home is never that cool, so keep them in the fridge.

Opening
You will need an oyster knife, a wet dishcloth and a tea towel. The knife should be solid, feel comfortable to hold and have a sturdy short blade. Always shuck at the last possible minute; once that abductor muscle is cut the oyster will die. Bury the oysters in crushed ice for 30 minutes before opening; they are easier to open when cold. Take your time opening them; don't rush, as that's when accidents will happen.

Secure a chopping board onto the work surface by placing the wet dishcloth underneath it for grip. Wrap the tea towel around an oyster, leaving the oyster hinge exposed. Insert the blade of the knife into the seal in the hinge where the top and bottom shells meet. Rock the knife until you have manoeuvred a gap in the two shells, then insert the blade a bit further to lever and push the knife into the hole in one controlled motion. Try to lift the top shell; once that has been achieved you can relax your grip a little. Finish lifting the top shell and then run the blade inside to release the oyster from the shell, leaving the oyster in the deep bottom shell. Discard the top shell.

Now, use the tip of the blade to go underneath the oyster to separate the abductor muscle from the shell – try to keep all of the oyster juice inside the shell when you do this. Use the blade to turn the oyster over for presentation. Serve immediately on a serving dish filled with crushed ice, to keep the oysters cool and to stop them falling over and spilling all that delicious oyster juice.

Grilled prawn cocktail.

This kitsch salad has made more comebacks than John Farnham...but in a good way! I have added lime, chilli and coriander (cilantro) as I love those flavours, so it's not a traditional prawn cocktail per se. Serve this as part of a shared table of dishes or plated individually.

Christmas timeline
Marinate the prawns the day prior and prep all the other elements of the salad, except for slicing the avocado. The prawns take no time to cook to order, and the salad is easy to arrange just before serving.

Serves
8 as part of a shared table

Prep time
15 minutes (plus minimum 4 hours marinating)

Cook time
15 minutes

1 bunch coriander (cilantro)
24 raw king prawns (jumbo shrimp), heads removed, peeled and deveined
80 ml (2½ fl oz/⅓ cup) olive oil, plus extra for drizzling
2 red bird's eye chillies, chopped with seeds
2 garlic cloves, finely grated with a microplane
finely grated zest of 1 lime
salt flakes
250 g (9 oz) cherry tomatoes
freshly ground black pepper
1 baby cos (romaine) lettuce, leaves removed, torn into large pieces
1 avocado, peeled and sliced
3 spring onions (scallions), peeled and thinly sliced diagonally
Cocktail sauce (page 2), to serve

1/ Pick the coriander leaves and wash well. Dry them using a salad spinner or pat dry with paper towel. Cut the stalks just above the roots and discard the roots. Wash the stalks and finely chop them. Reserve the leaves in the fridge.

2/ Put the prawns in a bowl with the oil, chilli, garlic, half of the lime zest, chopped coriander stalks and 2 teaspoons salt flakes. Mix well and leave to marinate for a minimum of 4 hours, or overnight to really get all those flavours in there.

3/ Preheat the oven to 150°C (300°F). Cut the tomatoes in half and place them on a baking tray, cut side up. Drizzle some olive oil over the top and season with salt and pepper. Put the tomatoes in the oven for 10 minutes to soften, then remove and set aside at room temperature.

4/ Heat a barbecue hotplate or preheat a grill (broiler) to high. Cook the prawns on the hot barbecue for 3 minutes, then turn them over and cook for a further 2–3 minutes. Slight charring and a just-cooked prawn is great – overcooking, not so great. Transfer the prawns to a plate. Now work on the salad.

5/ Arrange the lettuce leaves on a serving plate. Top with the avocado, tomatoes, coriander leaves and prawns. Sprinkle over the remaining lime zest and sliced spring onion. Serve with the cocktail sauce.

Gin-cured ocean trout w̲ blinis.

Anything gin and I am there! This is a neat way to incorporate this great drink into a delicious savoury starter. I used Four Pillars Navy Strength Gin here; however, you can use any gin you like, although a better quality gin will give a better outcome. You could also experiment a little here by using a flavoured gin.

Market
Fresh fish can be in short supply at Christmas, so avoid disappointment by placing a pre-order with your fishmonger a few weeks beforehand.

Christmas timeline
Prepare the trout on Christmas Eve after midday, for a perfect, lightly cured trout for Christmas Day nibbles. The blinis can be made up to 1 week in advance and frozen. Simply thaw, wrap in aluminium foil and heat in a warm oven.

Serves
8 as a starter; more as a snack

Prep time
10 minutes

Cure time
Overnight (or minimum 8 hours)

200 g (7 oz) salt flakes
200 g (7 oz) caster (superfine) sugar
1 teaspoon juniper berries, crushed
100 ml (3½ fl oz) gin
1 side ocean trout, about 1 kg (2 lb 3 oz), skin on
4 tablespoons chopped fresh dill
finely grated zest of 1 lime

To serve
Buckwheat blinis (page 39)
Quick pickled cucumbers (page 3)
Horseradish crème fraîche (page 3)

1/ To make the curing mixture for the trout, combine the salt, sugar and crushed juniper in a bowl. Stir in the gin and set aside.

2/ Lay a length of plastic wrap on the work surface. The plastic needs to be 50 per cent longer than the length of the fish. Lay down a second length, overlapping the two sheets to ensure the plastic is strong and wide enough. Spoon half of the curing mixture onto the centre of the plastic wrap and spread it out with a spoon so it covers an area about the same size as the fish.

3/ Place the side of trout, skin side down, onto the curing mixture. Spoon the remaining curing mixture over the flesh side of the trout. Enclose the plastic wrap around the fish, ensuring the curing mixture is covering the entire fish. Tightly wrap more plastic wrap around the trout and place on a tray in the fridge, skin side down. Place a board on top and weigh it down with something heavy to keep the fish flat. Leave to cure overnight.

4/ Remove the trout from the fridge and unwrap. Scrape off and discard the curing mixture, then use paper towel to brush the fish clean. Mix the chopped dill with the lime zest and press this on the surface of the fish.

5/ To serve, thinly slice the trout and serve on the blinis, with the pickled cucumber slices and horseradish crème fraiche.

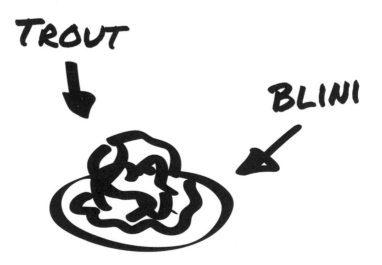

TROUT

BLINI

Buckwheat blinis.

Makes
30

Prep time
15 minutes

Cook time
15 minutes

150 g (5½ oz) unsalted butter
125 ml (4 fl oz/½ cup) warm
    full-cream (whole) milk
4 eggs, separated
100 g (3½ oz/¾ cup)
    buckwheat flour
50 g (1¾ oz/⅓ cup) plain
    (all-purpose) flour
7 g (¼ oz) salt
7 g (¼ oz) active dried yeast

1/ Melt 100 g (3½ oz) of the butter in the microwave, then leave to cool to room temperature. Put the warm milk in a bowl and whisk in the egg yolks.

2/ Sieve the flours into a bowl and add the salt and yeast. Mix well, then stir in the egg yolk and milk mixture followed by the cooled melted butter. Stir to form a smooth batter.

3/ Put the egg whites in the bowl of a freestanding electric mixer fitted with the whisk attachment. Whisk on medium speed until the egg whites start to foam, then add a pinch of salt and continue to whisk until soft peaks form.

4/ Gently fold the whisked egg whites into the batter using a large metal spoon or a silicone spatula. Once all the egg white lumps have been removed and you have a loose batter, the blinis are ready to cook.

5/ Wipe the base of a non-stick frying pan with the remaining butter and place the pan over medium heat. Place spoonfuls of batter into the pan and fry for a couple of minutes until bubbles appear on the surface. Turn them over using a small palette knife or spatula and cook the other side for 30–60 seconds until brown. Serve immediately.

Scotch quail eggs.

These wee scotch eggs are awesome as a canapé or even as a starter, and are also great with a chilled glass of sparkling.

Makes
12

Prep time
30 minutes

Cook time
20 minutes

12 quail eggs
450 g (1 lb) sausage meat
1 teaspoon fresh thyme leaves
2 garlic cloves, finely grated
salt flakes
freshly ground black pepper
3 eggs
150 g (5½ oz/1 cup) plain
(all-purpose) flour

150 g (5½ oz/2½ cups) panko
breadcrumbs
1 litre (34 fl oz/4 cups) canola
or sunflower oil for frying
Chilli mayonnaise (page 3),
to serve

1/ Using a slotted spoon, drop the quail eggs into a pan of boiling water and cook for 2 minutes. Remove the eggs and plunge into a bowl of iced water. Once cool, peel the eggs and set aside.

2/ Put the sausage meat and thyme and garlic in a bowl. Season with salt and pepper, mix well with clean hands, then divide the meat mixture into twelve equal portions.

3/ Take one portion of meat and flatten it out with your fingers, place a quail egg in the centre and then wrap it gently. Pinch to encase fully, ensuring there are no air pockets, and place on a tray. Repeat with the remaining eggs and meat mixture. Place the tray in the fridge for 1 hour.

4/ Whisk the eggs in a bowl. Put the flour in another bowl and put the breadcrumbs in a third bowl. Dip a scotch egg into the whisked egg, ensuring it is completed coated, drain off the excess, then coat first in the flour and finally in the breadcrumbs. Repeat with the remaining eggs. Give each egg a second coating of egg, flour and breadcrumbs. Refrigerate again for 15 minutes.

5/ Preheat the oven to 180°C (350°F). Heat the oil in a deep saucepan to 180°C (350°F); use a digital thermometer to check the oil temperature. Cook the eggs two at a time for 3 minutes, turning them in the oil, until crispy and golden brown. Drain on paper towel, then transfer to a baking tray. When the eggs are all done, put the tray in the oven for 4 minutes. Serve with the chilli mayonnaise.

Sides.

(+ SALADS)

Cheesy polenta <u>w</u> sweet corn.

This is superb straight from the pan, served with braised meats or the Turkey saltimbocca (page 64). Any leftovers can be poured into a baking dish and left to set overnight, then cut into pieces and fried the next day (see page 165).

Market
Fontina is a beautiful cheese and it works so well here. If you can't find it, don't stress – tallegio is just as good, or use any cheese you fancy.

Christmas timeline
This is best made fresh, so get organised and weigh all of your ingredients ahead of time, so it can be cooked easily when needed.

Serves
6

Prep time
5 minutes

Cook time
25 minutes

2 corn cobs, peeled
salt flakes
750 ml (25½ fl oz/3 cups)
  full-cream (whole) milk
100 g (3½ oz) unsalted butter
100 g (3½ oz) fine polenta
60 g (2 oz) parmesan, finely
  grated
100 g (3½ oz) fontina, chopped
  into cubes
1 tablespoon fresh thyme leaves
1 teaspoon ground white pepper

1/ To remove the kernels, stand the cobs on one end and use a sharp knife to slice downwards, as close to the cob as possible. Put the corn kernels in a glass or microwave-proof dish with a tablespoon of water and season with a pinch of salt. Microwave on High (100%) for 1 minute and set aside.

2/ Heat the milk and half the butter with a pinch of salt in a cast-iron or heavy-based saucepan over medium heat. Once it comes to the boil, slowly rain in the polenta while whisking constantly. Bring to the boil, stirring constantly, then reduce the heat to low and cook for 20 minutes, stirring every now and again. Be careful of hot splatters.

3/ Remove the pan from the heat and stir in the cheeses, remaining butter and corn kernels. Add the thyme and season with salt and white pepper, and continue to stir until all the cheese has melted. Serve immediately.

Brussels sprouts slaw.

What's worse than an overcooked brussels sprout? Not much! How can we make sure this never happens? That's right, DON'T cook them! The dressing is light and fragrant, making this dish so much more than reindeer feed. This is a great dish to serve with the Turkey saltimbocca (page 64).

Christmas timeline
Prepare the sliced vegetables for the slaw in the morning and get them in the fridge, with the dressing on the side, ready to dress at the last minute.

Serves
6–8

Prep time
20 minutes

Cook time
Nil

500 g (1 lb 2 oz) brussels
    sprouts, trimmed
1 large carrot, peeled
½ red onion
80 g (2¾ oz) radishes, trimmed
80 g (2¾ oz) wholegrain
    mustard
2 tablespoons white wine
    vinegar
juice of 1 lemon
100 ml (3½ fl oz) light olive oil
salt flakes
freshly ground black pepper
1 tablespoon chopped fresh
    flat-leaf (Italian) parsley

1/ Thinly slice the brussels sprouts to a 2 mm (⅛ in) thickness using a mandoline or sharp knife and add to a large bowl. Slice the carrot into long slices using the mandoline and then cut them into thin strips using a sharp knife. Add to the bowl with the brussels sprouts and mix well. Slice the onion half and radishes using the mandoline and add to the bowl.

2/ Combine the mustard, vinegar, lemon juice and oil in a bowl. Season to taste with salt and pepper, then pour the dressing onto the vegetables and toss. Adjust the seasoning if necessary, then stir in the parsley before serving.

Fried brussels sprouts w̲ white anchovy, walnut, garlic ± pecorino.

It's not Christmas lunch without brussels making an appearance. Thankfully the overcooked sprouts that have terrorised so many for so long have now gone. Rediscover brussels and their amazing versatility and flavour – there's so much you can do, just don't overcook 'em.

Market
Instead of buying them from the supermarket, visit your local market for the freshest, best quality sprouts you can find. After all, they are the star of this show.

Christmas timeline
For the best flavour, the brussels sprouts need to be fried just before you serve them, but you can get ahead by making the dressing the day before.

Serves
6–8

Prep time
10 minutes

Cook time
25 minutes

150 g (5½ oz) walnuts
80 ml (2½ fl oz/⅓ cup) light olive oil
80 ml (2½ fl oz/⅓ cup) walnut oil
2 tablespoons red wine vinegar
3 garlic cloves
1 lemon
salt flakes
freshly ground black pepper
vegetable oil for shallow frying
24 brussels sprouts
12–14 white anchovy fillets
75 g (2¾ oz) pecorino or parmesan

1/ For the dressing, preheat the oven to 150°C (300°F) and spread the walnuts on a baking tray. Roast for 15 minutes, then remove from the oven and set aside to cool. Leave the oven on.

2/ Put three-quarters of the nuts in a blender and blitz to a paste. Pour in the olive oil, walnut oil and vinegar, then use a microplane to finely grate in one of garlic cloves and the zest from half of the lemon. Mix well and season to taste with salt and pepper before transferring the dressing to a bowl. Hand chop the remaining walnuts and add to the dressing. If making the dressing ahead of time, store in a sealed container in the fridge.

3/ Remove any blemished leaves from the exterior of each brussels sprout, then cut the sprouts in half. Pour the vegetable oil into a frying pan to a depth of around 3 cm (1½ in) and heat over medium heat to 170°C (340°F); use a digital thermometer to check the oil temperature.

4/ Line a baking tray with paper towel. Add half of the brussels sprouts to the hot oil, cut side down, and fry for 4 minutes. Remove from the oil and lay them, cut side up, on the tray. Keep the sprouts warm in the oven while you fry the remaining sprouts.

5/ Thinly slice the remaining two garlic cloves and add them to the oil. Cook for 45 seconds, or until golden brown, then quickly remove them with a slotted spoon. Drain on paper towel.

6/ Arrange the fried sprouts on a serving dish and spoon over the walnut dressing. Add the anchovies and fried garlic. Finish by grating the pecorino and the zest from the remaining lemon half all over the dish.

Toasted sesame, honey ± yuzu carrot salad.

Veggie dishes are a real highlight for me when entertaining, and at Christmas you can go all out and try things you wouldn't normally cook. This simple dish of humble carrot is lifted into a new dimension by the tangy yuzu and toasted sesame. This salad goes well with most mains in this book, especially the Orange ± soy–glazed whole roasted duck (page 72).

Market
Yuzu is a type of Japanese citrus fruit. It can be hard to find, even in specialty markets, so I use bottled yuzu juice, which is found in most Asian supermarkets. Make sure you buy the pure unsweetened or salted variety.

Christmas timeline
If the weather is not too bad, and depending on what else I'm serving, I like to serve these at room temp. This means cook them before you serve your starters and they'll be fine to sit aside for a while.

Serves
6–8

Prep time
10 minutes

Cook time
10 minutes

2 bunches baby carrots, peeled and ends trimmed
120 g (4½ oz) unsalted butter
3 tablespoons sesame oil
2 tablespoons honey
2 tablespoons yuzu juice
2 tablespoons toasted sesame seeds

1/ Boil a large saucepan of salted water and blanch one bunch of carrots for 2 minutes. Remove from the water using tongs and place onto a plate. Repeat with the second bunch.

2/ Heat the butter and sesame oil in a non-stick frying pan over medium heat until the butter melts. Add the carrots and honey and cook for a few minutes, turning each carrot with tongs to glaze it in the honey and oil. Season with salt and continue to cook until they start to colour. Use tongs to transfer the carrots to a serving dish.

3/ Return the pan to the heat and heat the pan juices, then add the yuzu juice and stir to combine. Drizzle the dressing over the carrots and sprinkle with sesame seeds. Serve now, or later at room temperature.

Cucumber, zucchini ± fennel w goat's curd ± dill.

Here's something healthy and refreshing to help balance all the naughtiness. This is summer on a plate here in Oz, and these ingredients are abundant and in their prime, so go nuts. If you're from somewhere colder and can't find the range of zucchini and cucumbers listed here, then swap them for whatever is in season. You'll need to prepare this just before you serve it, but it's simple and quick and a mandoline makes short work of all the veg preparation – but if you don't have one, use a sharp knife.

Market
There are more cucumber varieties than just the usual suspects found in supermarkets. Support your local market and speak to producers to find new and exciting organic, heirloom and unusual varieties, to make this salad really stand out. While you're there, look for goat's curd in the deli section. Alternatively, buy it from specialty ingredient stores or cheese stores.

Serves
6–8

Prep time
20 minutes

Cook time
Nil

150 g (5½ oz) goat's curd
1 garlic clove, peeled
1 lemon
1 tablespoon pickling liquid
   from pickled cucumbers
   (see below)
2 tablespoons chopped dill
170 ml (5½ fl oz/⅔ cup) light
   olive oil
salt flakes
freshly ground black pepper
3 Lebanese (short) cucumbers
1 telegraph (long) cucumber,
   peeled
2 Japanese climbing cucumbers
1 zucchini (courgette)
2 yellow zucchini (courgettes)
1 batch Quick pickled
   cucumbers (page 3)
1 baby fennel bulb, fronds
   reserved

1/ For the dressing, put the goat's curd in a bowl. Use a microplane to finely grate the garlic clove and lemon zest into the bowl. Add the pickling liquid, chopped dill and 100 ml (3½ fl oz) of the oil. Season with salt and pepper and stir to combine.

2/ Use a mandoline to thinly slice all the cucumbers and zucchini to a 2 mm (⅛ in) thickness. For each type of cucumber and zucchini, slice them in different shapes. Cut the Lebanese cucumbers lengthways, the telegraph cucumber on a diagonal, and the Japanese cucumbers as rounds. Cut the green and yellow zucchini into long thin strips. Put the cucumber and zucchini in a large bowl and season with salt.

3/ Mix the remaining oil with the juice of the lemon and pour over the cucumbers and zucchini. Toss everything well and then add the pickled cucumbers.

 4/ Use the mandoline to thinly slice the fennel bulb, add to the bowl and toss everything again.

5/ Arrange the sliced vegetables on a serving platter and finish with the goat's curd dressing. Garnish with a few fennel fronds.

Broccolini w̲ anchovy ± lemon crumb.

This side dish is so delicious it could be a main event on its own! Crispy Turkish bread is the secret, and all of the other ingredients help to pack loads of flavour, too. This goes with anything really, but I have paired it with the Whole baked snapper w̲ chilli, lime, lemongrass ± coriander (page 88).

Market
I get my Turkish bread from my local baker, Tivoli Road, here in Melbourne, and it is so good! I urge you to support your local baker and get your bread from there rather than a supermarket. The difference in quality is amazing.

Christmas timeline
Cook this just before serving, so the bread chunks stay crunchy for longer.

Serves
6

Prep time
15 minutes

Cook time
20 minutes

150 g (5½ oz) Turkish bread
3 bunches broccolini
125 ml (4 fl oz/½ cup) light olive oil
25 g (1 oz) anchovy fillets in olive oil, chopped
2 garlic cloves, peeled
1 red bird's eye chilli, seeded and finely chopped
1 lemon
2 tablespoons finely chopped fresh flat-leaf (Italian) parsley
50 g (1¾ oz) pecorino or parmesan

1/ Tear the bread into bite-sized chunks and leave them to dry out.

2/ Bring a large saucepan of salted water to the boil and blanch the broccolini for 2 minutes. Drain, refresh the broccolini in cold water and then drain again.

3/ Heat half the oil and half the anchovies in a non-stick frying pan over medium heat. Use a microplane to finely grate the garlic cloves into the pan. Add the chilli and cook until the anchovies break down. Add the dried bread chunks and fry until golden brown. Remove from the pan.

4/ Heat the remaining oil in the pan, then add the broccolini and cook on all sides, turning the stalks regularly with tongs. Cook until they start to char on some sides. Grate in the lemon zest and then cut the lemon in half and squeeze in the juice from one of the halves. Stir in the parsley.

5/ Transfer the broccolini to a serving dish and add the crispy bread. Spoon the pan juices over the dish and grate some pecorino over the top.

Charred pea ± lettuce salad w̲ bacon, goat's cheese ± mint.

I love all of these ingredients, so why not put them all together? This salad will add freshness, colour and crunch to any celebration table, and the smokiness of the charred vegetables really takes this to a new level.

Market
Meredith goat's cheese is an amazing Australian product, with soft chunks of cheese marinated in garlic-infused oil. Try to find a similar product where you are, if this is not available to you.

Christmas timeline
This is a last minute one, as the ingredients will deteriorate once charred. To get a step ahead, you can cook the bacon in advance and reserve it at room temperature.

Serves
6–8

Prep time
15 minutes

Cook time
20 minutes

300 g (10½ oz) streaky bacon
60 ml (2 fl oz/¼ cup) light olive oil
3 baby cos (romaine) lettuces
salt flakes
freshly ground black pepper
250 g (9 oz) sugar-snap peas, trimmed
1 lemon, cut into 4 wedges
60 g (2 oz) baby English spinach, washed and dried
120 g (4½ oz) Meredith goat's cheese, crumbled
½ bunch mint, leaves picked

1/ Preheat the oven to 180°C (350°F) and line a baking tray with baking paper. Lay the bacon on the tray, drizzle with a little oil, then place in the oven and cook for 10 minutes, or until crispy. Transfer the bacon to a plate.

2/ Heat a barbecue grill plate or chargrill pan to high.

3/ Remove the outer leaves from each lettuce and discard them. Wash the lettuces and pat dry with paper towel. Cut each lettuce into quarters lengthways, toss with a little oil and season with salt and pepper. Place the lettuces onto the hot grill and cook for a couple of minutes, turning them so they char on all sides. Remove and set aside.

4/ Toss the sugar snaps in a bowl with a little oil, season with salt and pepper, then cook them on the grill until charred on each side. Remove and set aside. Finish by grilling the lemon wedges on each side to get them charred.

5/ Arrange the charred lettuce and sugar snaps, spinach, bacon and lemon wedges on a serving platter. Drizzle a touch more oil over the top, then crumble over the goat's cheese. Add the mint and serve.

Potato, leek, pancetta ± taleggio bake.

This is pure heaven and a great accompaniment to any roast. It's so easy to do as well; your guests will all want to recreate this when they get back in their kitchens.

Market
It's worthwhile making a trip to a cheesemonger to get taleggio – it's an amazing cheese. If it's not available, ask for fontina, or a recommendation for a suitable alternative.

Christmas timeline
Get the prep done the day before, layer everything into the dish and leave it covered in paper and foil in the fridge, so all you have to do is bake it on the day. Remove from the fridge for 1 hour beforehand so it can come to room temperature – this will ensure it cooks evenly.

Serves
6–8

Prep time
20 minutes

Cook time
1¾ hours

500 ml (17 fl oz/2 cups)
    thickened (whipping) cream
2 garlic cloves, peeled
1 bay leaf
salt flakes
freshly ground white pepper
75 g (2¾ oz) unsalted butter
4 leeks, white part only, sliced
100 ml (3½ fl oz) white wine
300 ml (10 fl oz) chicken stock
1 kg (2 lb 3 oz) dutch cream
    potatoes, peeled
8 thin slices mild pancetta
150 g (5½ oz) crème fraîche
canola oil spray
200 g (7 oz) taleggio

1/ Put the cream in a saucepan and finely grate in the garlic cloves using a microplane. Add the bay leaf and season with salt and white pepper. Bring to the boil over medium heat and once the cream has scalded, remove from the heat.

2/ Heat the butter in a large cast-iron pan over medium heat. Add the leek and a pinch of salt and stir. Cook for 5 minutes until the leek starts to soften and then deglaze the pan with the wine. Continue to cook until the wine has reduced by half, stirring occasionally, then add the stock. Again, cook until the liquid has reduced by half. Remove the pan from the heat and set aside.

3/ Preheat the oven to 180°C (350°F) and butter a 1.5 litre (51 fl oz/ 6 cup) pie dish. Use a slotted spoon to scoop out the leek from the pan and then spread the leek out to cover the base of the dish.

4/ Heat the remaining liquid left in the pan until boiling, then add the reserved cream infusion. Bring back to the boil and reduce the liquid by one-third. Strain the liquid through a sieve into a jug and set aside.

5/ Use a mandoline or sharp knife to slice the potatoes lengthways into a 2 mm (⅛ in) thickness. Cut one potato at a time, then, keeping the slices of each potato held together, use your fingers to fan out the potato into the dish, on top of the leeks. Arrange the slices lengthways around the outside edge and then slice and add more potatoes to start to fill in, to create a sliced spiral pattern.

6/ Add the pancetta, inserting the slices in between the potato, spacing them evenly apart. Pour the reserved cream over the potatoes and then use a teaspoon to distribute lumps of the crème fraîche on top.

7/ Cut out a disc of baking paper the same size as the dish. Lightly spray the paper with oil spray and lay the paper on top of the potato. Place a piece of aluminium foil to cover the top of the paper, and seal tightly to the dish.

8/ Transfer to the oven and bake for 1 hour. Remove the dish from the oven, then lift off and discard the foil and paper. Tear off small pieces of taleggio and push them into the cracks on the surface of the potato bake. Return the dish to the oven and bake for a further 25 minutes, uncovered, until the cheese has melted and the top is golden brown.

Cauliflower cheese.

Everyone loves this one – it's both naughty and nice! With its creamy, cheesy sauce, it's the perfect accompaniment to Beef wellington (page 67) or any roast.

Market
See a reputable cheesemonger for your gruyère as it is the perfect cheese for this. It melts well and has a beautiful nutty flavour. Alternatively, use an emmental, comté or even a cheddar instead.

Christmas timeline
You can prepare this dish the day before, up to the baking stage, so it's ready to go on the day. Remember to take it out of the fridge at least 30 minutes before baking so it cooks evenly.

Serves
4–6

Prep time
20 minutes

Cook time
45 minutes

1 large cauliflower, trimmed and
  cut into even-sized florets
50 g (1¾ oz) unsalted butter
50 g (1¾ oz/⅓ cup) plain
  (all-purpose) flour
500 ml (17 fl oz/2 cups) milk,
  warmed in the microwave
300 g (10½ oz) gruyère, grated
1 tablespoon wholegrain
  mustard
½ garlic clove, finely grated with
  a microplane
½ teaspoon white wine vinegar,
  or to taste
salt flakes
ground white pepper
½ bunch chives, snipped
1 egg yolk, lightly whisked

1/ Bring a large saucepan of water to the boil, season well with salt and blanch the cauliflower for 3 minutes. Drain, refresh the cauliflower in cold water and then drain again. Pour the blanched florets into a large baking dish.

2/ Preheat the oven to 200°C (400°F).

3/ Melt the butter in a large cast-iron pot or heavy-based saucepan over medium heat. Add the flour and stir for 2–4 minutes until light brown in colour. Gradually whisk in the milk and stir until the sauce starts to thicken. Bring to the boil, then reduce the heat to low and cook, stirring, for 3 minutes. Add two-thirds of the cheese, the mustard and garlic. Season to taste with the vinegar, salt and white pepper. Stir again and cook for a further minute before removing the pan from the heat.

4/ Stir the chives and egg yolk into the sauce, then pour the cheese sauce into the dish with the florets. Use a spoon to even out the sauce and make sure most of the cauliflower is coated. Sprinkle the remaining cheese over the top and bake in the oven for 30 minutes until golden brown. Serve immediately.

Pork, leek, sage ± fennel stuffing.

It's not Christmas without stuffing! This simple side dish is quick to knock up but not short on flavour. It goes well with a traditional roast turkey or the Turkey saltimbocca (page 64), and the raw mix can be used to stuff a bird for all-in-one roasting.

Market
Visit your butcher to buy good-quality sausages made from free-range pork.

Christmas timeline
Make this stuffing up to 3 days in advance and store in the fridge uncooked. Bake fresh on the day.

Serves
6–8

Prep time
20 minutes

Cook time
55 minutes

50 g (1¾ oz) unsalted butter
50 ml (1¾ fl oz) olive oil
2 French shallots, finely chopped
2 leeks, thinly sliced
1 garlic clove, finely grated with a microplane
1 kg (2 lb 3 oz) pork and fennel sausages, casings removed
1 teaspoon fennel seeds, toasted and ground
4 tablespoons finely chopped fresh sage
2 tablespoons finely chopped fresh flat-leaf (Italian) parsley
1 tablespoon finely chopped fresh dill
finely grated zest of ½ lemon
250 g (9 oz/2½ cups) dried breadcrumbs
1 teaspoon salt flakes
1 teaspoon ground white pepper

1/ Preheat the oven to 180°C (350°F). Heat the butter and oil in a large heavy-based saucepan or cast-iron pot over medium heat until foaming. Add the shallots, leek and garlic and reduce the heat to medium–low. Cook for 10 minutes to sweat down the vegetables, stirring regularly.

2/ Scrape the contents of the pan into a large bowl. Add all the remaining ingredients, then use clean hands to mix everything until well combined.

3/ Transfer the mix into a 2 litre (68 fl oz/8 cup) baking dish and push down to level. Bake for 45 minutes, or until golden brown and cooked.

Duck-fat roasted potatoes.

The duck fat makes these roasted potatoes ridiculously naughty – worthy of your Christmas table for sure. Crispy and crunchy with fluffy centres, the secret to success is in using fresh potatoes, parboiling them and then leaving them to dry out, which all help to produce a crispier spud.

Market
Any kind of roasting or floury potato will work well here, but you need to make sure they are really fresh. Buy them from your local market or greengrocer as close to Christmas Day as possible. Duck fat can be bought from a good butcher or specialist ingredient shop.

Christmas timeline
Parboil the potatoes on Christmas Eve, then leave them to dry overnight in the fridge.

Serves
4–6

Prep time
10 minutes (plus minimum 4 hours drying)

Cook time
About 2 hours – long enough to watch *The Muppet Christmas Carol*

2 kg–2.5 kg (4 lb 6 oz–5½ lb) king edward, desiree or sebago potatoes, washed (peeled if preferred)
30 g (1 oz) salt
150 g (5½ oz) duck fat
salt flakes

1/ Cut the potatoes into even roast potato size. Put them in a large saucepan, cover with cold water and add the table salt. Bring to the boil over medium heat and cook for about 15 minutes, or until they are soft all the way through. Drain and return the potatoes to the saucepan. Give them a shake to roughen up the edges, which will crisp up beautifully when roasted.

2/ Pour the potatoes onto a tray and pat dry with paper towel. Put the tray in the fridge to dry out for a minimum of 4 hours but preferably overnight.

3/ Preheat the oven to 180°C (350°F) and line a deep ovenproof dish or baking tin with baking paper that comes about 2 cm (¾ in) up the sides. This ensures the duck fat does not run under the paper and stays close to the potatoes when roasting.

4/ Put the duck fat into the dish and place in the oven to heat up for 10 minutes. Remove the dish from the oven and add the potatoes, using tongs or a spoon to coat each potato in the melted duck fat. Sprinkle the potatoes liberally with salt flakes. Return the dish to the oven and cook for up to 1½ hours, shaking and turning the potatoes every 30 minutes. Serve hot.

Showstoppers.

Turkey saltimbocca.

Take a break from tradition and do something different this year. Better than a boring old roast, this is a lot easier to get right as well. Get the prep done ahead of time and your guests will be impressed with the no-stress lunch, cooked and on the table in no time. This is great with Cheesy polenta w sweet corn (page 44) and Brussels sprouts slaw (page 45).

Market
Free-range heritage-breed turkeys will taste so much better than something from the supermarket, so go and see your poultry expert at the market. Ask your butcher to slice super thin pieces of pancetta for you as well.

Christmas timeline
Prep the turkey and wrap it in pancetta on Christmas Eve. Leave it in the fridge overnight, then remove 30 minutes before cooking. Make the sauce after you cook the bird, then pour yourself a glass of wine and bask in the glory of nailing a turkey lunch. Simples!

Serves
6

Prep time
25 minutes

Cook time
40 minutes

1 x 1.5 kg (3 lb 5 oz) turkey breast fillet
freshly ground black pepper
16 fresh sage leaves
12 large, thin, round slices mild pancetta
125 ml (4 fl oz/½ cup) light olive oil
4 French shallots, thinly sliced
pinch of salt flakes
150 ml (5 fl oz) dry white wine
185 ml (6 fl oz/¾ cup) chicken stock
¼ lemon
60 g (2 oz) unsalted butter, chilled and diced

1/ Trim the turkey breast and cut it into twelve equal-sized pieces. Cover each piece with a piece of plastic wrap and flatten it by pounding with a meat mallet or rolling pin.

2/ Season each piece with pepper only (no salt at this point), and then place a sage leaf on top of each one. Reserve the remaining four leaves for the sauce. Wrap a slice of pancetta around each piece of turkey, covering the sage and holding it in place.

3/ Preheat the oven to 160°C (320°F). Line a baking tray with baking paper.

4/ Heat 2 tablespoons of the oil in a large frying pan over medium–high heat. Add four pieces of saltimbocca to the pan, placing them sage side down. Cook for 4 minutes before turning them over and cooking for a further 4 minutes. Transfer to the prepared tray.

5/ Cook the remaining turkey pieces, four at a time – you don't need to clean the pan between each batch. Transfer the tray and turkey pieces into the warm oven, then turn the oven off.

6/ To make the sauce, heat the remaining oil in the pan over low heat. Add the shallots, a few grinds of pepper and a pinch of salt and gently sauté the shallots for 5 minutes. Increase the heat to medium and deglaze the pan with the wine, scraping the base of the pan to incorporate any bits stuck on the bottom. Cook until the wine has reduced by half, then add the stock and again reduce this by half.

7/ Squeeze in a few drops of lemon juice and add the remaining sage leaves. Bring to the boil, then whisk in the butter, a cube at a time, until you have a smooth and shiny sauce.

8/ Arrange the turkey pieces on a platter or divide among individual plates and serve with the sauce.

Beef wellington.

This is an absolute winner of a dish and it will really show off your skills as a cook. Getting the 'doneness' of the meat correct while ensuring crispy puff pastry is the real trick to success. Don't let this put you off though; use a digital thermometer to make sure you can carve in front of your guests with absolute confidence that you've nailed it.

Market
Ask your butcher for a ready-to-go trimmed piece of beef fillet. Tell him what you are doing with it, so he can give you a piece that is a similar width along its length.

Christmas timeline
You can prep this up to a day ahead and cook it on the day Just remember to remove the beef from the fridge at least 1 hour before cooking – the beef needs to be at room temperature so it cooks evenly.

Serves
6

Prep time
40 minutes (plus chilling)

Cook time
about 1 hour

800 g (1 lb 12 oz) mushrooms, such as button, portobello, flat, swiss or a mix
salt flakes
freshly ground black pepper
1 tablespoon chopped fresh thyme
1 garlic clove, peeled
1 tablespoon chopped fresh tarragon
1.25 kg (2 lb 12 oz) beef fillet, trimmed, at room temperature
80 ml (2½ fl oz/⅓ cup) olive oil
3 tablespoons dijon mustard
15 thin slices rolled pancetta
flour for dusting
750 g (1 lb 11 oz) block puff pastry or 2 x 375 g (13 oz) sheets (see Chef's note)
3 egg yolks
1 tablespoon cream

Chef's note
Make your own or use a store-bought puff pastry block and roll to your own shape and thickness. Otherwise, use pastry sheets; I like to use Carême puff pastry, which comes in 375 g (13 oz) sheets. You can lay two sheets on top of each other and roll them out to the size you need; this is better than rolling them separately and then trying to seal them together.

1/ Put half the mushrooms in a food processor, season with salt and pepper, and pulse to a course paste. Scrape into a bowl. Repeat with the remaining mushrooms and add to the bowl. Add the thyme and grate in the garlic clove using a microplane, then stir to combine.

2/ Place a large non-stick frying pan over medium heat and add half the mushroom paste. Cook, stirring constantly, until all of the moisture has evaporated and the paste looks dry. Transfer to a container and repeat with the remaining mushrooms. Chill the mushroom paste in the fridge and, once cold, stir in the tarragon.

3/ Heat a large heavy-based frying pan over medium heat. Rub the beef fillet with the oil and then rub a generous amount of salt flakes into the surface of the meat. Once the pan is hot, add the fillet and sear the flesh for 30 seconds on each side, and then sear both ends, using tongs to move and turn the beef in the pan. This will seal the meat ready for wrapping. Place the beef on a tray and brush or rub the mustard all over it before putting it in the fridge to cool for 30 minutes.

4/ Lay two sheets of plastic wrap on the work surface, overlapping them if necessary to make a rectangle large enough to wrap the beef. Lay the pancetta slices on the plastic wrap, slightly overlapping each other (three slices wide and five slices long) to form a rectangle large enough to cover the beef.

5/ Spoon the chilled mushroom paste onto the pancetta and spread it evenly to cover. Place the beef fillet into the middle and then use the plastic wrap to help wrap the fillet with the mushroom and pancetta. Form a tight tube and tie a knot in one of the ends of the plastic. Roll the beef, using one hand to hold the untied end of plastic wrap. Roll tight and tie a knot in the other end to secure. Place in the fridge for a minimum of 1 hour to set and firm up.

6/ Meanwhile, lightly dust the work surface with flour. Use a rolling pin to roll the block or sheets of pastry to a 5 mm (¼ in) thickness, in a rectangle large enough to wrap the meat. If using two pastry sheets, place one on top of the other and roll them together to stick before rolling out to the larger size.

7/ Make an egg wash by mixing the egg yolks with the cream and a pinch of salt. Mix well with a fork.

8/ Unwrap the beef and lay it in the centre of the pastry rectangle. Use a sharp knife to cut out squares of excess pastry from the four corners of the rectangle. Reserve one pastry square to use later for decoration, and use the remaining trimmings for something else (such as the Mango tarte tatin, page 122). Brush the reserved piece of pastry with the egg wash and put it in the fridge to chill.

9/ Wrap the beef by first pulling the longer end pieces of pastry over the ends of the beef towards the centre and then pulling over the larger side pieces towards each other, to completely enclose the beef. Brush the pastry with egg wash and seal the pastry pieces together.

10/ Turn the wellington over so the pastry seal is underneath and place it on a baking tray. Brush the pastry completely with egg wash, then place the beef in the fridge to set for 15 minutes. Brush the top with egg wash again and leave to set in the fridge for a further 15 minutes. Repeat this step a third time for a super egg-washed welly.

11/ Preheat the oven to 200°C (400°F). Use a toothpick, skewer or knife to score the wellington in evenly spaced lines, first one way across and then the other, to form a diamond pattern. Use a 2 cm (¾ in) round pastry cutter to cut a small circular hole in the top of the wellington, to let out steam during cooking. Cut a 4 cm (1½ in) diameter circle from the reserved pastry piece and then cut out a 2 cm (¾ in) circle from the centre of this disc. Place the pastry ring on the top of the wellington, to collar the hole at the top.

12/ Place the beef in the oven and cook for 30 minutes. Turn the tray around, reduce the temperature to 180°C (350°F) and cook for up to a further 30 minutes, or until the internal temperature of the beef reaches 55°C–60°C (131°F–140°F) for medium-rare to medium. Use a digital or meat thermometer to test this.

13/ Remove from the oven and allow the beef to rest for 10 minutes before transferring to a board for carving either at the table or in the kitchen.

YOU DID IT!

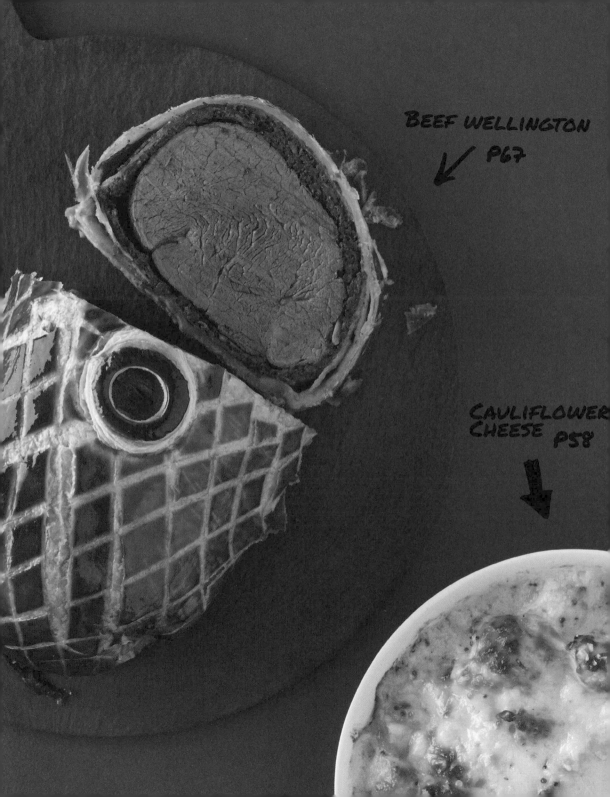

BEEF WELLINGTON
P67

CAULIFLOWER
CHEESE P58

Duck-Fat Roasted Potatoes P60

Fried Brussels Sprouts w White Anchovy, Walnut, Garlic + Pecorino P46

Orange ± soy–glazed whole roasted duck.

Roast duck just screams 'celebration' and you can celebrate the right way by serving this to your loved ones. It's sweet and sour, shiny and sticky and oh so utterly delicious (see pic page viii). This is surprisingly easy to do, but plan ahead for the best results.

Market
Visit your butcher for a good-quality duck and ask him to prep it by removing the head and feet, so it's ready for roasting. You can make your own duck stock if you ask your butcher to keep the trimmings from your duck; otherwise, buy a good-quality duck stock from the butcher, or poultry or ingredient stores.

Christmas timeline
Cook this fresh to order for superstar results, but you can prep ahead. Brine the duck the night before and prepare all the ingredients for the glaze, so you're ready to go on the day. The brining process will help pull the skin taut and gives a professional finish and flavour to your dish.

Serves
4

Prep time
20 minutes (plus overnight brining)

Cook time
1 hour 10 minutes or the first half of *Die Hard*; you can watch the rest after lunch

1 x 1.8 kg–2 kg (4 lb–4 lb 6 oz)
   whole duck
4 oranges
16 cloves
1 garlic bulb
500 ml (17 fl oz/1 cups)
   duck stock
100 ml (3½ fl oz) hoisin sauce
100 ml (3½ fl oz) kecap manis
3 tablespoons soy sauce
1 tablespoon honey
4 star anise
20 g (¾ oz) julienned ginger

Brine
2.75 litres (93 fl oz/11 cups)
   water
100 g (3½ oz) salt
50 g (1¾ oz) caster (superfine)
   sugar
4 star anise
1 tablespoon black peppercorns
1 tablespoon Chinese five-spice

1/ For the brine, combine the water, salt, sugar, star anise and peppercorns in a large saucepan over medium heat, stirring regularly to dissolve the salt and sugar. Bring to the boil, then remove from the heat.

2/ Open the cavity of the duck and sprinkle the five-spice inside. Put the duck into a large container or bowl. Pour enough brine over the duck to cover, then place a small plate or weight on top, to ensure the bird remains submerged. Refrigerate overnight.

3/ The next day, remove the duck from the brine and pat dry with paper towel. Discard the brine and store the duck in the fridge for a minimum of 4 hours to dry out further.

4/ Remove the duck from the fridge 45 minutes before cooking. Preheat the oven to 200°C (400°F).

5/ Cut one orange in half, stud the two halves with the cloves and then stuff both orange halves into the cavity of the duck. Put the duck into a roasting tin. Cut two oranges into quarters and cut the top off the garlic bulb and add them to the tin. Keep the cut-off part of the garlic for the glaze.

6/ Cut strips of zest off the remaining orange, then juice the orange. Put the zest and juice in a saucepan with the stock, garlic trim, hoisin, kecap manis, soy sauce, honey, star anise and ginger. Bring to the boil over high heat and cook until the glaze has reduced by two-thirds.

7/ Brush the hot glaze all over the duck and then pour the remaining glaze over the duck. Transfer to the oven and roast for 30 minutes. Remove from the oven, brush the duck with the combined pan juices and glaze, then return to the oven and cook for a further 35 minutes. Remove from the oven and baste with the glaze again, repeating this process every 5 or 6 minutes until you have a beautiful roasted and glazed bird.

8/ Bring the whole duck to the table to carve. Serve with the roasted orange quarters and drizzle over any pan juices.

Mud crab <u>w</u> ginger, spring onion ± sesame.

OMG this dish is Ah-mazing – a real luxury. It's not a traditional Chrissy Day main, but I'd choose this over turkey every time.

Market
Try to source live cleaned mud crabs and please kill them humanely (see Chef's note, page 77). You can use other varieties of crab for this, depending on what you have available near to you – ask your fishmonger about ordering ahead. And remember, this is a luxury (read 'expensive') item, especially at Christmas.

Christmas timeline
This needs to be one of the last things cooked on Christmas Day so, to minimise stress and workload, make sure the other items on your menu are things that can be prepared in advance. For example, serve a pre-glazed ham and salads with this and a trifle for dessert. See my sample menus on pages x–xi for suggestions.

Serves
4–8 depending on other food served

Prep time
15 minutes (plus freezing)

Cook time
15 minutes

2 x 1.5 kg (3 lb 5 oz) live mud crabs, cleaned
4 tablespoons potato starch
400 ml (13½ fl oz) vegetable oil
250 ml (8½ fl oz/1 cup) chicken stock (or shellfish or vegetable stock)
100 g (3½ oz) ginger, peeled and thinly sliced
1 garlic clove, finely grated on a microplane
10 spring onions (scallions), trimmed and thinly sliced
pinch of salt flakes
3 tablespoons shaoxing rice wine or dry sherry
3 tablespoons sesame oil

To garnish
2 large red chillies, thinly sliced
2 tablespoons toasted sesame seeds

1/ To prepare the crabs humanely, put them in the freezer for at least 35 minutes to make sure they are no longer alive. Remove the crabs from the freezer. Lift the abdominal flap underneath, pull it to remove and discard. Hold the bottom end of the large top shell and pull it away. Pull off and discard the gills and use your fingers to scoop out and discard any internal bits. Twist off the two large claws on each crab and crack them with the back of a heavy knife. Cut the body of each crab in half lengthways with the legs attached, then cut each section through the body again into two pieces. Lightly dust all the crab pieces with half of the potato starch.

2/ Heat the vegetable oil in a large wok over medium heat to 170°C–175°C (340°F–345°F); use a digital thermometer to check the oil temperature. Add two crab claws and cook for 2–3 minutes until they turn red – take care of spitting oil. Remove the claws and reserve, then cook the remaining two claws the same way. Pour the hot oil into a separate pot and set aside to cool.

3/ Mix the remaining potato starch with 4 tablespoons of the stock and reserve.

4/ When the wok has cooled down, wipe it clean with paper towel. Add 2 tablespoons of the cooled oil to the wok (you can discard the rest) and heat over medium heat. Add the ginger, garlic and three-quarters of the spring onion. Stir-fry for 1 minute, then add the crab pieces and the remaining stock. Season with the salt, give it a mix, then cover with the lid and simmer for 5 minutes.

5/ Remove the lid, add the reserved potato starch mixture and stir in well. Add the shaoxing wine and sesame oil and heat through.

6/ Arrange the crab on a platter and pour the sauce over the top. Garnish with the remaining spring onions, chilli and sesame seeds.

Seafood platter.

The showstopper to end all showstoppers! What a statement you're making with this. It's not cheap though, but it is Christmas. You really can choose whatever you want for your own platter, depending on availability and what you like – just make sure you have enough of everything so no one misses out on anything. Melted butter for the crab is a must, as are finger bowls, claw crackers and picks – and lots of napkins. Now all you'll need are a few bottles of (very) chilled dry white wine.

Market
Pre-order your seafood to avoid disappointment. Although there is a recipe here, talk to your fishmonger and ask what's best on the day. For example, if the oysters are spawning and not great for consumption, the fishmonger will be able to suggest another alternative.

Christmas timeline
To get a head start, cook the seafood on Christmas Eve and then chill everything overnight in the fridge for an easy assembly on Christmas Day.

Serves
6 as a main; more as a starter

Prep time
30 minutes

Cook time
15 minutes

18 oysters, preferably unshucked

1 x 2 kg (4 lb 6 oz) cooked or live crayfish (see Chef's note)

18 raw king prawns (jumbo shrimp), heads removed, peeled and deveined

1 kg (2 lb 3 oz) live mussels, cleaned and debearded

1 cooked mud crab, claws cracked

450 g (1 lb) Cocktail sauce (page 2)

300 g (10½ oz) Mignonette sauce (page 29)

300 g (10½ oz) salted butter, melted

2 lemons, each cut into 4 quarters

baby cos (romaine) lettuce leaves, to serve

12 small wholemeal (wholewheat) bread rolls

Chef's note
If you are planning on killing any live seafood for consumption, then please kill humanely. The following link is helpful for this: http://kb.rspca.org.au/What-is-the-most-humane-way-to-kill-crustaceans-for-human-consumption_625.html

1/ If your oysters are unshucked, open them up about 45 minutes before you are ready to serve everything (see page 32).

2/ Cut the crayfish in half and split open. Scoop out any unwanted bits and pull out the tail meat. Wash the shell and chop the tail meat into large pieces and place back into the shell.

3/ Preheat a barbecue hotplate or chargrill pan over high heat. Alternatively, preheat the grill (broiler) to high. Cook the prawns for 3 minutes, then turn them over and cook for a further 2–3 minutes. You want the prawns to be slightly charred and just cooked through – take care not to overcook them or they'll be rubbery. Reserve on a plate.

4/ Place a large shallow pan, such as a flameproof casserole dish, on the stovetop and heat on high for 4 minutes. Tip in the mussels and cover with a lid to steam them open. Cook for 3–4 minutes and then remove from the heat. Use tongs to transfer the mussels to a plate and refrigerate.

5/ Buy your crab cooked and serve as they are with crackers and picks. Or pick the crab ahead of time for your guests and serve in a crab dish.

6/ Pile lots of crushed ice onto a large platter and arrange all the chilled and cooked items on top. Serve with the sauces, melted butter, lemon wedges, lettuce and bread, and away you go.

Pork rack <u>w</u> crispy crackling.

Just a simply done, beautifully cooked piece of pork. Oh, but that crackling though! They won't be missing the turkey, that's for sure.

Market
The pork is the star of the show here, so ask your butcher for the best quality free-range pork that he has. Or better still, buy direct from a farmer at a farmers' market.

Christmas timeline
Marinate early on Christmas Eve to get those flavours right in there, then rub off the marinade early on Christmas Day. Then leave the pork to dry out for a few hours, giving more chance for that crackling to shine.

Serves
8

Prep time
15 minutes (plus overnight marinating and 1 hour resting)

Cook time
about 1¾ hours

1 tablespoon fennel seeds, toasted and ground
3 garlic cloves, finely grated with a microplane
2 tablespoons chopped fresh sage
1 tablespoon chopped fresh thyme
200 ml (7 fl oz) olive oil
3 kg (6 lb 10 oz) pork rack with bones
salt flakes
freshly ground black pepper
Apple sauce (page 2), to serve

1/ Put the fennel seeds, garlic, sage, thyme and oil in a bowl and mix together.

2/ Using a sharp knife, make 4 mm (½ in) deep score lines into the pork skin, spacing the score lines about 3 mm (⅛ in) apart. Take the fennel seed mixture and rub it all over the pork. Transfer the pork to a dish and season all over with salt and pepper. Wrap the dish really well in plastic wrap and refrigerate overnight.

3/ Preheat the oven to 190°C (375°F). Line a roasting tin with baking paper. Remove the pork from the fridge and use paper towel to wipe off the marinade and dry the pork really well. Make sure you clean and dry well in between the scored marks on the skin. Leave to come to room temperature for 1 hour.

4/ Liberally rub more salt into the skin and scored grooves, then place the pork, skin side down, into the prepared tin. Roast for 1¼–1½ hours, or until the internal temperature of the pork reaches 55°C (131°F); use a digital thermometer to check the temperature.

5/ Remove the pork from the oven and turn the rack over so it is skin side up. Turn the grill (broiler) on high and return the pork to the oven, on the middle rack, with the oven door open. Cook for 5–8 minutes until the skin is crispy. Remove from the oven and rest for 15 minutes before serving. Serve with the apple sauce.

Pineapple ± mustard–glazed ham.

'Rock Star Ham' they should call it! Cos that's what you're gonna be when you bust this out on Chrissy Day.

Market
See a reputable butcher for your ham and order ahead of time so you don't miss out. I usually order mine early to mid-November from my friend and top butcher, Gary McBean. Make sure your ham is free range and lightly smoked. If you are unsure about removing the rind and scoring the fat, and if you have a great relationship with your butcher, they may be able to take care of this task for you.

Christmas timeline
Make the pineapple jam way ahead, in November even, and store it in the fridge.

Serves
1 large impressive glazed ham

Prep time
15 minutes

Cook time
about 1½ hours – or nearly the whole of *Home Alone*

1 x 8 kg–9 kg (17 lb–20 lb) whole smoked leg ham
200 g (7 oz) Soft-set pineapple jam w lime, vanilla ± star anise (page 156)
100 g (3½ oz) soft light brown sugar
2 tablespoons dijon mustard
whole cloves

1/ Prepare your ham for glazing by first removing the outer rind. Use a sharp knife to cut around the shank of the ham, about 10 cm (4 in) from the end. Run the knife around the rind and underneath the skin, then remove it in one piece by running your fingers between the rind and the fat. Trim some of the excess fat on the surface of the ham if it is too thick, but ensure you leave a layer of fat to protect the meat during glazing.

2/ Using a sharp knife, carefully score the fat in an even diamond pattern, about 2 mm (⅛ in) deep. Stud the centres of each of the diamonds with a clove. Place the ham on a large baking tray lined with baking paper.

3/ Preheat the oven to 180°C (350°F) and remove all of the oven shelves except the lowest shelf.

4/ Put the pineapple jam, sugar and mustard in a bowl and stir to combine well. Brush half of the glaze onto the scored side of the ham. Place the ham in the oven and leave to glaze for 35 minutes. Remove from the oven and brush the remaining glaze onto the ham; cook for a further 15 minutes. Remove and then use a spoon to baste the ham with the juices and melted glaze; cook for a further 15 minutes. Repeat this step twice more for a further 30 minutes total cooking time. Remove the ham from the oven.

5/ Let the ham rest and cool down in the tray for 30 minutes, then transfer to a serving board. At the last minute, brush some of the excess juices onto the exterior of the ham to give it a lovely sheen.

6/ Grip the shank end of the ham like a handle and use a long, thin, very sharp knife to carve. Start by cutting a wedge of meat halfway into the ham and reserve, then cut thin slices to expand the cavity, ensuring each slice has some of the glaze.

BROCCOLINI
W ANCHOVY +
LEMON CRUMB
P52

Whole baked snapper w̲ chilli, lime, lemongrass ± coriander.

Maximum effect with minimum effort, this table showstopper will not disappoint – and really, it's dead easy! Serve with steamed rice and Broccolini w̲ anchovy ± lemon crumb (page 52).

Market
So you can be sure you'll get the size you want and the freshest fish you can, speak to your fishmonger a couple of weeks before Christmas about placing an order.

Christmas timeline
The fish needs to be prepped and marinated overnight, so on the day all you have to do is simply pop it in the oven.

Serves
6

Prep time
25 minutes (plus overnight marinating)

Cook time
50 minutes

1 x 2.5 kg–3 kg (5½ lb–6 lb 10 oz) snapper, cleaned and scaled
30 g (1 oz) peeled ginger
6 garlic cloves, peeled
3 limes
2 kaffir lime leaves, thinly sliced
10 spring onions (scallions), trimmed, white part only, thinly sliced
3 red bird's eye chillies, chopped with seeds
2 large red chillies, sliced with seeds
1 lemongrass stem, white part only, thinly sliced
3 tablespoons fish sauce
3 tablespoons light soy sauce
100 ml (3½ fl oz) light olive oil
1 bunch coriander (cilantro), roots washed and chopped (reserve leaves for garnish)
1 tablespoon salt flakes
1 tablespoon freshly ground black pepper

1/ Take a sharp knife and make six to eight diagonal incisions into the skin along the mid section of the fish, about 1 cm (½ in) apart. Turn the fish over and repeat on the other side, then transfer the fish to a large dish.

2/ Use a microplane to grate the ginger, garlic and lime zest into a bowl. Juice the limes into the bowl and then add the remaining ingredients. Mix well. Rub the mixture all over the fish and inside the fish cavity, making sure you get the marinade into the incisions in the skin. Cover and refrigerate overnight.

3/ Remove the fish from the fridge and transfer it to a baking tray lined with baking paper. Leave the fish to rest at room temperature for 30 minutes.

4/ Preheat the oven to 200°C (400°F). Bake the fish for 50 minutes, or until the flesh is white and pulls apart when tested with a fork. Garnish with the reserved coriander leaves and serve with bowls of steamed rice.

JUST...ONE...MORE

Desserts
± cheese.

(OH, SWEET)

Mince pies.

My record in a year is 16,000 – that's made not eaten, cheeky! That was at The Savoy in London, where I made around 120 mince pies a day, starting in August to ensure I had enough for the December onslaught! I've done my best to scale down my recipe for you here.

Market
For the mince pie filling, try to use beautiful organic local dried fruit and the best quality alcohol you can.

Christmas timeline
There are two parts to this recipe: the filling and the pastry. You'll need to start the filling about 2 weeks beforehand, to allow time for the fruit to macerate (you could even start earlier than that and leave the fruit to soak for up to 1 month). If you like, prepare your mince pies the day before and bake them on the day, or freeze them uncooked (wrap the tins in plastic wrap or store in a container in the freezer). You can bake them from frozen, but increase the cooking time to 28–30 minutes.

Makes
24

Prep time
20 minutes (plus resting time for dough)

Cook time
24 minutes

480 g (1 lb 1 oz) unsalted butter, at room temperature
1 vanilla bean, seeds scraped
finely grated zest of 1 orange
2 teaspoons salt
300 g (10½ oz) icing (confectioner's) sugar, sieved
3 eggs
1 egg yolk
800 g (1 lb 12 oz/5⅓ cups) plain (all-purpose) flour
100 g (3½ oz/1 cup) ground almonds
canola oil spray
1 quantity Mince pie filling (page 94)
Whipped brandy orange butter (page 8), to serve

Egg wash
3 egg yolks
2 tablespoons cream
pinch of caster (superfine) sugar, plus extra for sprinkling
pinch of salt flakes

1/ Put the butter, vanilla seeds, orange zest, salt and icing sugar in the bowl of a freestanding electric mixer fitted with the paddle attachment. Cream the ingredients on low speed until pale and smooth, scraping down the inside of the bowl with a spatula to ensure the butter is evenly mixed.

2/ Add the eggs, one at a time, beating well, then add the egg yolk and mix until incorporated. Scrape down the bowl again.

3/ Add the flour and ground almonds and mix until the dough just comes together. Turn the dough out onto a lightly floured work surface and knead it briefly for 30–60 seconds. Divide the dough into two pieces and flatten them down. Cover each piece in plastic wrap and rest in the fridge for 1 hour.

4/ Preheat the oven to 180°C (350°F). Lightly spray your tart tins or moulds (see Chef's note, below) with oil spray.

5/ Remove both pieces of pastry from the fridge and lightly flour the work surface. Use a rolling pin to roll out one pastry disc to a 3 mm (⅛ in) thickness. Using an 8.5 cm (3¼ in) round cutter, cut out 24 discs for the base. Roll out the second pastry disc and use a 7.5 cm (3 in) round cutter to cut out 24 discs for the lids. Reroll the pastry scraps if needed. Any leftover pastry can be wrapped and frozen for another time.

6/ Push the larger pastry discs into each tart tin, using your fingers to push the pastry to the edges of the tins. Spoon the mince pie filling into each lined tart, filling it to the top. Store any excess filling in the fridge for another time.

7/ Take the smaller discs of pastry and lay it on top of the filling. Use your thumb and forefinger to pinch the lid to the base. Use a small knife to trim off any excess pastry.

8/ For the egg wash, combine the egg yolks, cream, sugar and salt in a bowl. Brush some of the egg wash over the top of each mince pie and sprinkle with some extra sugar. Place the mince pies on a baking tray and bake for 24 minutes or until golden brown. Serve with Whipped brandy orange butter.

Chef's note
I use 6 cm (2½ in) non-stick mince pie tins for these at home, but at the studio I use aluminium foil tart tins, which work really well and allow me to freeze the mince pies uncooked in the tins, ready for baking.

Mince pie filling.

Prep time
30 minutes (plus minimum
2 weeks for marinating)

Cook time
Nil

180 g (6½ oz/1¼ cups) currants
220 g (8 oz/1¾ cups) raisins
200 g (8 oz) sultanas (golden raisins)
100 g (3½ oz/½ cup) mixed peel (mixed candied citrus peel), chopped
100 g (3½ oz) glacé ginger in syrup, cut into 5 mm (¼ in) dice
100 ml (3½ fl oz) brandy
100 ml (3½ fl oz) rum
100 ml (3½ fl oz) pedro ximénez
200 g (7 oz) Apple compote (page 9)
60 g (2 oz) muscovado sugar or soft light brown sugar
80 g (2¾ oz) flaked almonds, lightly toasted
40 g (1½ oz) walnuts, chopped
finely grated zest and juice of 2 oranges
1 teaspoon ground cinnamon
1 teaspoon ground allspice

1/ Put the currants, raisins, sultanas, mixed peel and glacé ginger in a plastic container that has a lid. Mix the ingredients well, then pour in the brandy, rum and pedro ximénez. Mix again and cover with the lid. Leave the fruit at room temperature for at least 1 week (or up to 1 month), mixing the fruit every day to make sure the fruit soaks evenly.

2/ Add the remaining ingredients to the container and mix well. Again, leave covered at room temperature for a minimum of 1 week, mixing every day. Store covered in a container in the fridge for up to 2 months, or transfer to sterilised jars for longer storage (up to 1 year).

Hot banana, rum ± raisin caramel puddings w̱ chocolate sauce

I know it's really cold in Europe and the US at Christmas, but it's not always that warm here in Oz either. I remember my first Christmas 'down under' and it was freezing. I was working on Christmas Day and I remember looking out the kitchen door and seeing hailstones the size of golf balls. Wish I had a bowl of this on that day.

Christmas timeline
To get on top of everything, you need to start this recipe by soaking the raisins in the rum. They'll need to soak for a minimum of 4 hours before you can begin the other components of the recipe.

Serves
8

Prep time
40 minutes (plus 4 hours soaking raisins)

Cook time
40 minutes

Rum ± raisins
125 ml (4 fl oz/½ cup) dark rum or spiced rum
250 g (9 oz/2 cups) raisins

Banana ± rum caramel sauce
150 g (5½ oz/²/₃ cup) caster (superfine) sugar
reserved rum liquid (drained from raisins)
1 overripe banana, mashed with a fork
pinch of salt
25 g (1 oz) unsalted butter
1 firm banana, cut into 24 thin slices

1/ For the rum and raisins, heat the rum in a small saucepan until just below boiling point. Remove the pan from the heat and add the raisins. Cover with the lid and leave to cool and plump up at room temperature for a minimum of 4 hours. Drain the raisins, reserving the liquid for the caramel sauce. Chop the raisins and set aside.

2/ For the caramel sauce, place a non-stick frying pan over medium heat. When the pan is hot, add the sugar and cook, stirring with a wooden spoon, until the sugar turns to a caramel. Once you have a dark amber caramel, deglaze the pan by slowly adding the reserved rum from the raisins. Stir to combine before adding the mashed banana. Boil and whisk the sauce together, then add the salt and cook for 1 minute. Remove from the heat and whisk in the butter. Set aside.

3/ Lightly grease eight 200 ml (7 fl oz) ramekins. Alternatively, bake the puddings in a muffin tray or as one large pudding in a 1.5 litre (51 fl oz/6 cup) dish. Pour the caramel sauce evenly into the base of each ramekin, then arrange three pieces of banana over the caramel. Set the ramekins aside while you prepare the sponge.

Sponge.

200 g (7 oz) unsalted butter,
  at room temperature
100 g (3½ oz) caster (superfine)
  sugar
100 g (3½ oz) muscovado sugar
  or soft light brown sugar
2 vanilla beans, seeds scraped
4 eggs

4 overripe bananas, mashed
  with a fork
320 g (11½ oz) self-raising flour
2 teaspoons bicarbonate of
  soda (baking soda)
100 ml (3½ fl oz) full-cream
  (whole) milk
Hot chocolate sauce (page 7),
  to serve

1/ Preheat the oven to 180°C (350°F).

2/ Put the butter, both sugars and vanilla seeds in the bowl of
a freestanding electric mixer fitted with the paddle attachment.
Cream the ingredients on low–medium speed for 8–10 minutes
until smooth and pale, scraping down the inside of the bowl with
a spatula to ensure the butter is evenly mixed.

3/ Add the eggs, one at a time, beating continuously. Add the
mashed banana and mix well.

4/ Sieve the flour and bicarbonate of soda into a bowl. Turn the
machine to low, add the flour to the bowl followed by the milk
and reserved chopped raisins and beat until combined.

5/ Using a spoon, divide the batter evenly among the caramel
and banana ramekins, then tap the moulds to level.

6/ Bake for 25 minutes, or until risen and golden. Remove from
the oven and turn the puddings out into serving bowls, making
sure the sauce covers the pudding. Serve with the chocolate
sauce on the side.

On chocolate.

Working with chocolate
When doing anything chocolate related, you need to make sure you are working in a cool environment – an air-conditioned room set to 18°C (64°F) is ideal. Ensure your work surfaces and equipment, such as bowls, palette knives and spatulas, are meticulously clean. It's also worthwhile investing in a digital thermometer. Store any unused chocolate in a sealed plastic container in the pantry.

Melting chocolate
I prefer to use the microwave to melt all of my chocolate under 2 kg (4 lb 6 oz) in quantity, as I find it easier to control. To melt chocolate in the microwave, follow these simple steps:

1/ Choose a clean microwave-safe bowl – a plastic or glass bowl is ideal.

2/ Add the chopped chocolate or melts (buttons) to the bowl, place in the microwave and heat on High (100%) for short bursts at a time. Remember, the microwave CAN burn your chocolate, so heat the chocolate for up to 30 seconds at a time, and stir in between each burst of heat to ensure an even temperature throughout.

3/ Melt the chocolate until it reaches around 45°C (113°F); use a digital thermometer to accurately check the temperature.

Tempering chocolate
Melted chocolate is great for simple preparations, but if you want to dip or coat an item in chocolate or make decorations, then you must first temper the chocolate to ensure it has a crisp outer shell and doesn't melt in your hand.

1/ To temper chocolate, follow steps 1 and 2 for Melting chocolate (see left), but remove the bowl from the microwave when only half of the chocolate has melted.

2/ Stir the chocolate vigorously. The residual heat will melt the remaining chocolate, but if you are having trouble with the last few lumps, then place the bowl in the microwave for 5 seconds at a time, or melt the lumps quickly with a hair dryer. Use as directed in the recipe.

Chocolate shards
These are an easy garnish that will make your Christmas trifle or cake look amazing.

1/ Temper the chocolate (see left) and pour a small amount onto a piece of baking paper. Top with another piece of paper and use a rolling pin to roll the chocolate thinly.

2/ Place the sheets in the fridge. Once set, peel away the paper and break the chocolate into shards. Store in a sealed plastic container until needed. These can be made in advance and stored in a cool, dark place or in the fridge.

Christmas trifle.

It simply is not Christmas without a trifle; it makes such a great table centrepiece. The best thing is you can invent your own trifle layers using your favourite sponge or meringue – mix and match fruits, creams, jellies and inclusions – there really are no rules. This trifle is entirely made up of recipes from this book.

Market
Just go for it! I'm using cherries here because they are AMAZING but use whatever you fancy as a fruity substitute.

Christmas timeline
The best part about this, apart from the taste, is that it can all be made in advance. Knock this out on Chrissy Eve and you'll be winning.

Serves
12–16

Assembly time
25 minutes (plus overnight setting and 1 hour chilling on the day)

500 g (1 lb 2 oz) Cherries in vanilla syrup (page 134)
500 ml (17 fl oz/2 cups) Moscato jelly (no raspberries) (page 105)
720 g (1 lb 9 oz) White chocolate + vanilla cream, whipped (page 8)
2 x Chocolate brownie discs, 18 cm (7 in) diameter (page 140)
75 g (2¾ oz) dark chocolate, melted (see page 98)
360 g (12½ oz) Custard (page 6)
200 g (7 oz) Champagne sabayon (page 6)

To decorate
fresh cherries
Cherries in vanilla syrup, extra, drained
Meringue dots (page 102)
dark chocolate shards (see page 98)
edible gold leaf

1/ For the trifle, you will need a 2.5 litre (85 fl oz/10 cup) glass bowl with a diameter of 18–20 cm (7–8 in) to fit all the layers.

2/ Drain the cherries and reserve the syrup. Arrange the cherries in the bottom of the glass bowl. Slowly pour the melted jelly into the bowl to cover the cherries. Place the bowl in the fridge and leave to set overnight.

3/ The next day, spoon half of the white chocolate and vanilla cream onto the jelly and spread it out to the edge of the bowl with a spoon. Drizzle half of the reserved cherry syrup over the top of the cream.

4/ Place one of the chocolate brownie discs on top of the cream and push it gently into the cream layer to half submerge it. Spoon the remaining white chocolate and vanilla cream onto the chocolate sponge. Drizzle the melted chocolate over the top using a spoon.

5/ Place the second chocolate brownie disc on top of the cream and again push it gently into the cream layer to half submerge. Spoon on the custard and spread it out to the edge of the bowl before drizzling the remaining cherry syrup over the top.

6/ Spoon the champagne sabayon over the custard, to fill the glass bowl. Refrigerate for a minimum of 1 hour to let everything settle and soak in.

7/ Meanwhile, prepare the decorations for the trifle. Make the meringue dots and chocolate shards.

8/ When you are ready to serve, remove the trifle from the fridge. Decorate with fresh cherries, drained cherries in syrup, meringue dots, chocolate shards and gold leaf.

Meringue dots.

Prep time
15 minutes

Cook time
2 hours

2 egg whites
135 g (5 oz) icing
    (confectioners') sugar
food colouring as required

1/ Put the egg whites and icing sugar in the bowl of a freestanding electric mixer.

2/ Fill a saucepan three-quarters full with water and sit the bowl (with the egg whites and sugar in it) over the top of the pan, ensuring the base of the bowl isn't touching the water.

3/ Turn the heat to medium. The water will start to gently heat the egg mixture. Whisk constantly so the meringue mixture does not overcook and coagulate, and heat until the meringue mix is hot to the touch.

4/ Remove the bowl from the pan and place it into the electric mixer and attach the whisk. Whisk on high speed until you have a thick and glossy meringue. At this point you can colour or flavour the meringue however you like. I used a water-soluble purple food colouring for my meringues to garnish the trifle.

5/ Preheat the oven to 80°C (175°F). Get out a large baking tray or use two trays. Transfer the mixture to a piping (icing) bag fitted with a 1 cm (½ in) plain tip and pipe four small dots of meringue into each corner of the tray. Place a sheet of baking paper on the tray and stick the corners down with the meringue dots.

6/ Pipe the meringue in neat rows of small 'bulbs', evenly spaced apart, onto the baking paper. Pipe each bulb slowly with steady pressure to a small bulb size; release the pressure before lifting the tip up from each bulb to get a pointed end.

7/ Place the tray in the oven and bake for 1 hour. Open the oven and rotate the tray, then turn the oven off and close the door. Leave the meringues in the oven for another hour and they should be cooked and crispy. Allow to cool before storing in a clean, dry container or biscuit tin.

Peanut butter s'mores.

Now we are putting Santa's cookie dough to even better use with these gooey, nutty and decadent marshmallowy bites.

<u>Makes</u>
10

<u>Prep time</u>
30 minutes

<u>Cook time</u>
20 minutes

600 g (1 lb 5 oz) Santa's
    chocolate chip cookie dough,
    uncooked (page 137)
5 gold-strength gelatine leaves
2 egg whites
75 ml (2½ fl oz) water
200 g (7 oz) caster (superfine)
    sugar

1 teaspoon liquid glucose
150 g (5½ oz) peanut butter,
    smooth or crunchy
200 g (7 oz) dark chocolate,
    melted (see page 98)

1/ Preheat the oven to 180°C (350°F). Line two large baking trays with baking paper.

2/ Divide the dough into twenty balls, each weighing 30 g (1 oz). Place the balls on the trays, spacing them apart, and cook for 14 minutes. Remove from the oven and press each cookie down slightly with the base of a saucepan. Transfer the cookies to a wire rack to cool down.

3/ For the marshmallow, soak the gelatine leaves in a bowl of cold water for 2 minutes to soften.

4/ Put the egg whites in the clean bowl of a freestanding electric mixer fitted with the whisk attachment. Start to whisk the egg whites on low speed.

5/ Meanwhile, put the water, sugar and glucose in a small saucepan over medium heat. Stir gently to dissolve the sugar and bring the syrup to the boil. Cook the syrup until it reaches 140°C (284°F); use a digital or sugar thermometer to check the temperature.

6/ Once the glucose syrup has reached the correct temperature and is boiling, turn the mixer with the egg whites to medium speed. Slowly pour the syrup onto the whisking egg whites – pour in a constant stream down one side of the bowl to avoid the whisk. Reserve the hot saucepan. Once all of the syrup has been added, turn the mixer to high speed and continue to whisk.

7/ Drain the gelatine and gently squeeze out the excess water. Add the soaked gelatine to the hot saucepan. The residual heat in the pan will melt the gelatine. Slowly pour the liquefied gelatine into the mixing bowl and continue to whisk the marshmallow for 5 minutes on a high speed until it starts to cool and thicken.

8/ Lay ten cookies out onto a tray, flat side up, and place a teaspoon of peanut butter onto each one. Spoon a tablespoon of marshmallow on top of the peanut butter. Top each one with the remaining cookies, placing them flat side down. Flick melted chocolate onto the cookies, stack them on a plate and serve.

Moscato ± raspberry jelly.

A real showstopper and so easy to whip up. Now Uncle Matty won't be the only wobbly one at the table! You can serve the jelly in individual moulds or glasses, but I love the drama of a large one. Set it in a beautiful dish and pair it with fruit, cream or ice cream – or all of them – for pure indulgence. I'd probably serve the kids something else, though, as it's quite potent.

Market
I'm using raspberries because I love them, but most fruits would work: peach slices, cherries, strawberries or a combination of all of them.

Christmas timeline
Make the jelly the day before. Don't leave it too late – you don't want a sloppy mess as your table centrepiece.

Serves
6–8

Prep time
30 minutes (plus setting times for each layer)

Cook time
5 minutes

20 gold-strength gelatine leaves (see Chef's note, below)
250 ml (8½ fl oz/1 cup) cold tap water
2 x 750 ml (25½ fl oz) bottles moscato or pink sparkling wine
500 g (1 lb 2 oz) caster (superfine) sugar
500 g (1 lb 2 oz) fresh raspberries
fresh raspberries, Vanilla sauce (page 7) or Champagne sabayon (page 6), to serve

1/ Soak the gelatine leaves in a shallow container with the cold water for 4 minutes to soften.

2/ Meanwhile, heat the moscato and sugar in a saucepan over medium heat. Turn the heat off just before the mixture starts to simmer. Stir to dissolve the sugar but don't whisk, as you don't want air bubbles in the mix. Add the gelatine and water mixture to the hot liquid in the pan and stir gently to melt the gelatine. Strain the jelly through a sieve into a large jug or bowl.

3/ Add the gelatine and water mixture to the hot liquid in the pan and stir gently to melt the gelatine. Strain the jelly through a sieve into a large jug or bowl.

4/ Pour a quarter of the jelly into a 3 litre (101 fl oz/12 cup) jelly mould. Use any shape you like. Place the jelly in the fridge to start to set. Keep checking the jelly and when it has just set but is still wobbly (after around 1 hour), remove from the fridge and scatter a quarter of the raspberries over the surface of the jelly.

5/ Top up with another quarter of the jelly mix and again place in the fridge to set, then scatter another quarter of the raspberries over the top. Repeat this step twice more, to use all of the jelly and raspberries. Place in the fridge, preferably overnight, to fully set.

6/ Top with additional berries and serve with vanilla sauce or Champagne sabayon.

Chef's note
I always use leaf gelatine and prefer gold strength, but don't stress if you can't find that. You need about 45 g (1½ oz) of gelatine leaves for this recipe, so if you have bronze, titanium or silver gelatine leaves, that's fine, just use 45 g (1½ oz). If you are using powdered gelatine, then read the back of the pack to work out how much you will need to set around 2.25 litres (76 fl oz/ 9 cups) of liquid.

Gingerbread-spiced pumpkin pie.

A twist on the much-loved American holiday dessert, made using a non-traditional method. Instead of a smooth, set pumpkin custard pie, this is more textured but just as delicious. And…spoiler alert…chefs do use a microwave! Here 'Chef Mike' helps us produce an easy and great-tasting filling that is all pumpkin! Enjoy y'all.

Market
Pumpkin is pretty much available all year round, so why wait for Christmas? You can enjoy this pie any time of year and it is fun to serve at Halloween or Thanksgiving as well. Gingerbread spice, also known as lebkuchen spice mix (and similar to pumpkin pie spice sold in the US), is available from specialty ingredient shops.

Christmas timeline
Fresh is always best chef, but if you are pushed for time then this pie will freeze well.

Serves
8–10

Prep time
60 minutes (allows for chilling pastry)

Cook time
45 minutes (plus 45 minutes for the filling) – plenty of time to knock over *The Nightmare Before Christmas*

150 g (5½ oz) unsalted butter, at room temperature
135 g (5 oz) caster (superfine) sugar
pinch of salt
1 egg
1 egg yolk
320 g (11 oz) self-raising flour, sieved
2 tablespoons gingerbread spice
1 quantity Pumpkin filling (page 110), cooled

To finish
1 egg yolk
4 tablespoons milk
sprinkle of caster (superfine) sugar
Vanilla sauce (page 7), to serve (optional)

1/ Put the butter, sugar and salt in the bowl of a freestanding electric mixer fitted with the paddle attachment. Cream the ingredients on low speed for 8–10 minutes until pale and smooth, scraping down the inside of the bowl with a spatula to ensure the butter is evenly mixed.

2/ Add the egg and egg yolk and mix well, then add the sieved flour and gingerbread spice. Continue to mix for 30 seconds until the dough comes together.

3/ Cut four 40 cm (16 in) square pieces of baking paper. Divide the dough in half. Using a rolling pin and lots of flour to prevent sticking, roll out one piece of dough between two squares of paper. Working quickly as the dough is very soft, roll it out until it is about 1 cm (½ in) thick and roughly fits the size of the paper. Place the sheet of pastry into the fridge and repeat with the remaining dough and two pieces of paper. Chill both sheets of pastry in the fridge for a minimum of 30 minutes.

4/ Preheat the oven to 170°C (340°F). Lightly grease a 22.5 cm (9 in) ceramic pie dish.

5/ Take one of the sheets of pastry from the fridge. Quickly remove both pieces of baking paper and use your fingers to start pressing the pastry into the pie dish. Work as fast as you can, as the pastry goes soft very quickly. Don't worry if it tears or there are holes; this pastry is forgiving and you can just use your fingertips to push the pastry in to cover any holes. Line the base and up the side of the dish with the pastry.

6/ Add the cooled pumpkin filling and smooth it out with a spatula or spoon.

7/ Take the other sheet of pastry out of the fridge and again quickly remove the pieces of baking paper. Make a lid for the pie, pressing the pastry to the edge of the dish with your fingers.

8/ To finish, make an egg wash by whisking the egg yolk and milk in a small bowl. Lightly brush this over the top of the pie and sprinkle with the sugar. Bake for 40–45 minutes, rotating the dish halfway through cooking. Leave to cool for 20 minutes before slicing and serving from the dish. Serve either warm or cold, with vanilla sauce if you like.

P118 →
BARBECUED
SPICED
PINEAPPLE
WEDGES

PEANUT
BUTTER
S'MORES

P103 ↓

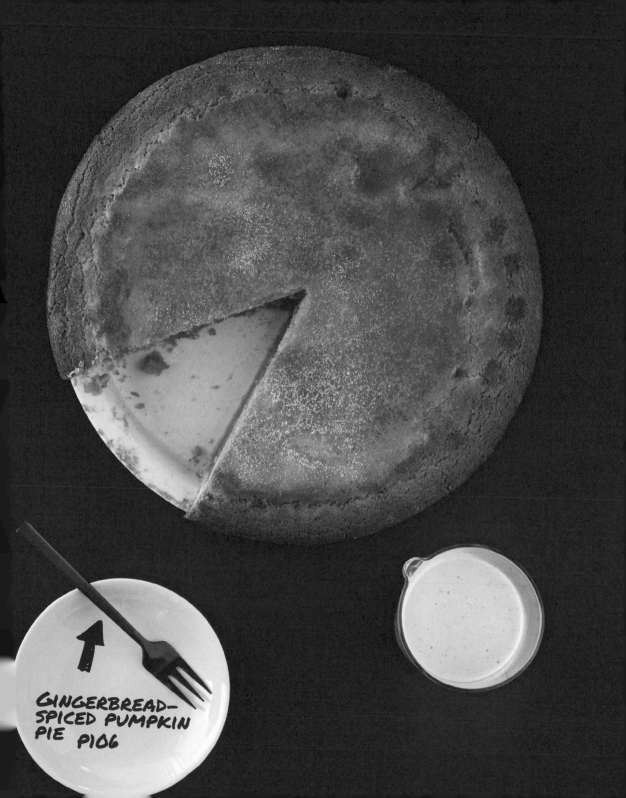

GINGERBREAD-
SPICED PUMPKIN
PIE P106

Pumpkin filling.

Prep time
10 minutes

Cook time
45 minutes

1.5 kg (3 lb 5 oz) peeled
  pumpkin (winter squash)
1 vanilla bean, seeds scraped
finely grated zest and juice of
  1 orange
175 g (6 oz/¾ cup) caster
  (superfine) sugar
½ teaspoon freshly grated
  nutmeg
½ teaspoon ground cinnamon
½ teaspoon ground ginger

1/ Cut the pumpkin into similar-sized chunks and put in a large microwave dish (with a lid that allows the steam to escape). Cook in the microwave on High (100%) for 20 minutes. Drain off any water from the pumpkin.

2/ Add the vanilla bean and seeds, orange zest and juice, sugar and spices to the pumpkin and return to the microwave. Cook on high for a further 20–25 minutes, stirring the filling every 5 minutes to ensure even cooking. Remove from the microwave and stir until smooth. Leave to cool completely before filling the pie.

Pavlova.

This is one of THE most iconic of desserts of all time – at least here in Oz and especially during the summer. Pav can be a bit temperamental, so you'll need a couple of practice goes so you can learn how your oven bakes and then gauge cooking times to ensure success. It'll be worth it though, to see their faces at Christmas lunch when you bring this beauty to the table. Take a bow, chef …

Market
I love the classic passionfruit pavlova – just cream and fresh passionfruit – though I do often add fresh mango pieces and even a few strawberries. Whatever you fancy, though, just nothing overly sweet, as the pav is sweet enough.

Christmas timeline
Do not underestimate the pav! It's not tricky to make once you have practised it a couple of times, but you do need a bit of patience. I like to cook it on Christmas Eve after dinner and then just leave it in the oven overnight to cool.

Serves
8–10

Prep time
30 minutes

Cook time
50 minutes (plus minimum 5 hours cooling)

6 egg whites, at room temperature
½ teaspoon cream of tartar (see Chef's note, below)
1 vanilla bean, seeds scraped
pinch of salt
400 g (14 oz) caster (superfine) sugar
2 teaspoons cornflour (cornstarch)
2 teaspoons white vinegar
400 ml (14 fl oz) thickened (whipping) cream
12 passionfruit, cut in half, pulp scooped out
icing (confectioners') sugar, for dusting

1/ Preheat the oven to 150°C (300°F). Line a heavy baking tray with baking paper. Ensure the oven fan is turned off. Take a 20 cm (8 in) diameter cake tin or ring and place it in the middle of the paper; use a pencil to draw a circle around the tin. Flip the paper so the drawn ring is underneath.

2/ Put the egg whites, cream of tartar, vanilla seeds and salt in the bowl of a freestanding electric mixer fitted with the whisk attachment. It's important that the bowl is immaculately clean and dry or the egg whites won't whisk properly. Whisk the egg whites on medium speed until foamy, then add the sugar, 1 tablespoon at a time. Continue beating until all but 50 g (¾ oz) of sugar has been incorporated – this should take about 15 minutes. Turn the machine to high and whisk for a further 5 minutes.

Chef's note
Cream of tartar is added to the egg whites to create a creamy consistency; it is available from most large supermarkets.

3/ Mix the cornflour into the remaining sugar and fold into the meringue using a silicone spatula or large metal spoon. Ensure the cornflour mixture is fully incorporated before folding in the vinegar.

4/ Spoon the meringue into the centre of the circle on the lined paper. Use a palette knife to shape and compress the meringue into a large dome shape. Next, start to push the meringue out to the edges of the circle, smoothing the top at the same time. You are trying to obtain a thick disc of pavlova-shaped meringue. Indent the centre top surface of the meringue with the palette knife to create a small lip around the top edge of the meringue.

5/ Place the tray on the middle shelf of the oven and immediately reduce the temperature to 100°C (200°F). Bake the pavlova for 50 minutes. Turn the oven off and leave the pavlova to cool in the oven for a minimum of 5 hours. The pav should be crunchy on the outside and soft and marshmallowy in the centre – a little browning on the exterior is perfect, as that is what holds it and gives it its crunch. Remove from the oven and gently remove the paper from the base.

6/ Whip the cream to firm peaks and spoon it onto the centre of the pav, spreading it out to the edges. Spoon the passionfruit pulp over the top.

The Christmas pudding.

Christmas timeline
I make my puddings for my shop around July, and cook them then as well. I store them in the fridge and reheat by steaming them in the oven for a couple of hours on the day. Easy!

Serves
6–8

Prep time
30 minutes

Cook time
5 hours (plus 1½ hours reheating)

150 g (5½ oz/1 cup) plain (all-purpose) flour
½ teaspoon ground ginger
½ teaspoon ground cinnamon
½ teaspoon ground allspice
½ nutmeg, freshly grated (or ½ teaspoon ground nutmeg)
30 g (1 oz) dried breadcrumbs
30 g (1 oz) unsalted butter, at room temperature
70 g (2½ oz) soft light brown sugar
20 g (¾ oz) ground almonds
½ teaspoon salt
100 g (3½ oz) sultanas (golden raisins)
40 g (1½ oz) currants
100 g (3½ oz) raisins
45 g (1½ oz) dried cranberries
30 g (1 oz) dried pears, chopped
50 g (1¾ oz) dried apricots, chopped
100 g (3½ oz) mixed peel (mixed candied citrus peel), chopped

1 carrot, peeled and coarsely grated
1 apple, peeled and coarsely grated
50 g (1¾ oz) glacé ginger, cut into 5 mm (¼ in) dice
50 g (1¾ oz/⅓ cup) blanched almonds, toasted and roughly chopped
finely grated zest and juice of 1 orange
finely grated zest and juice of 1 lemon
1 tablespoon milk
1 egg
25 ml (¾ fl oz) cognac
25 ml (¾ fl oz) whisky
25 ml (¾ fl oz) rum
50 ml (1¾ fl oz) pedro ximénez
25 ml (¾ fl oz) muscat
75 ml (2½ fl oz) port
100 ml (3½ fl oz) Guinness
75 ml (2½ fl oz) brandy (to flambé)
Brandy custard (page 6), to serve

1/ Sieve the flour and spices together into a large mixing bowl. Add the breadcrumbs and rub in the butter using your fingertips until all the butter has been incorporated. Add the brown sugar, ground almonds and salt and mix well.

2/ Add all the remaining ingredients in the order they appear above, except the brandy, and mix well with a spatula.

3/ Grease a 1.2 litre (41 fl oz) pudding basin (mould) and pour in the batter. Push down to completely fill the bowl and eliminate any air bubbles. Cut a disc of baking paper to fit the diameter of the base of the pudding and lightly grease it. Place the paper, greased side down, to cover the pudding, then wrap the entire pudding in aluminium foil.

4/ Preheat the oven to 150°C (300°F). Put the pudding basin in a cast-iron pot. Fill the pot with enough hot water to come halfway up the side of the pudding. Cover the pot with a lid and cook in the oven for 5 hours, checking the water level every hour and topping it up as needed. Alternatively, cook the pudding in an oven that has a steam function. Cook in a 100°C (200°F) oven for 5 hours.

5/ Remove from the oven and leave to cool. You can leave the pudding in the basin and cover with plastic wrap or aluminium foil and store in the fridge until needed – it will keep for up to 1 year!

6/ To reheat on the day, repeat one of the cooking methods above, leaving it in the oven for a good 1½ hours.

7/ Heat the brandy in a microwave for 10 seconds. Turn the pudding out onto a serving dish, remove the disc of baking paper, and pour over the brandy. Set it alight and take a bow. Serve with brandy custard.

BRANDY
CUSTARD
P6 →

THE CHRISTMAS
PUDDING
← P114

COFFEE-INFUSED
RUM + DARK
CHOCOLATE TRUFFLES

P152

SALTED
CARAMELS
P154

MINCE
PIES

P92

Barbecued spiced pineapple wedges.

Here in Oz, getting the barbecue going on Christmas Day is one of life's great pleasures. But don't fret if you're somewhere cold and want to make these – cook them on the stovetop in a chargrill pan or even in a saucepan.

Market
Pineapples work extremely well here as they are robust and won't break up on the grill, and their sweet yet tart flavours work beautifully with the other flavours in the dish. You could use bananas as an alternative.

Christmas timeline
Make the caramel marinade and marinate the pineapple, and buy a tub of coconut ice cream on Christmas Eve and that's the hard work done!

Serves
4

Prep time
10 minutes (plus overnight marinating)

Cook time
10 minutes

1 large pineapple
2 star anise
10 cloves
2 cinnamon sticks
20 black peppercorns
300 g (10½ oz) caster (superfine) sugar
2 vanilla beans, seeds scraped
2 red bird's eye chillies, chopped with seeds
20 g (¾ oz) peeled ginger
2 overripe bananas, mashed with a fork
100 ml (3½ fl oz) malibu, bacardi or rum (or a mix)
50 g (1¾ oz) unsalted butter
½ teaspoon salt
store-bought coconut ice cream, to serve

1/ Peel the pineapple, then use a sharp knife to cut it in half lengthways. Cut each half into four wedges and trim off the core if you don't want to eat it (I personally don't mind it). Place the pineapple wedges in a dish and set aside.

2/ Put the star anise, cloves, cinnamon sticks and peppercorns into a pestle and mortar or a small spice grinder and pulverise until coarsely ground – it doesn't have to be a ground to a fine powder.

3/ Place a non-stick frying pan over medium heat. When the pan is hot, add the sugar and cook, stirring, until the sugar turns to a caramel. Once you have a dark even-coloured caramel, reduce the heat to low and add the vanilla seeds and chilli, then use a microplane to grate in the ginger. Stir well and cook for 1 minute before adding the ground spices. Stir again and increase the heat to medium.

4/ Add the mashed banana and stir, then slowly add the alcohol and stir to combine. Cook for a couple of minutes and remove from the heat.

5/ Whisk in the butter and salt and pour the mix into a blender. Blitz the caramel for 1 minute on medium speed and then strain the sauce onto the pineapple wedges. Leave to marinate overnight.

6/ Preheat the barbecue to high. Drain the pineapple, reserving the sauce. Cook the pineapple wedges for 5 minutes on one side, then turn them over and cook for 3 minutes on the other side. Slide onto plates, drizzle over some of the reserved sauce, and serve hot with coconut ice cream.

Muscat ± raisin ice cream sandwiches.

They'll be rockin' around the Christmas tree with these festive treats. You could buy a good-quality vanilla ice cream and soften it slightly before folding in the alcoholic fruits if you don't have access to an ice cream machine.

Market
The wine regions of Rutherglen and Glenrowan, here in Victoria, are where muscat is produced. It is a delicious dark and sticky fortified wine, which works so well at Christmas. It's a bit like madeira, so you can use that or dark rum if you can't find muscat.

Christmas timeline
Don't try to make everything on one day. Make the cookies and store them in a tin, and get the ice cream base made the day before. Don't forget to soak those raisins early as well.

Makes
10 ice cream sandwiches

Prep time
30 minutes (plus overnight soaking and 3½ hours freezing)

Cook time
5 minutes

175 ml (6 fl oz) muscat
160 g (5½ oz/1¼ cups) raisins
650 ml (22 fl oz) Vanilla sauce (page 7), made the day before
20 Santa's chocolate chip cookies (page 137)
300 g (10½ oz) milk chocolate, melted (see page 98)

1/ Heat the muscat in a small saucepan over medium heat until it just starts to simmer. Remove the pan from the heat and add the raisins. Cover with plastic wrap and leave to cool and infuse at room temperature overnight, or for at least 12 hours.

2/ Pour the cold vanilla sauce into an ice cream maker or churner and follow the manufacturer's instructions to churn fresh ice cream.

3/ Drain the raisins, reserving the soaking liquid. Chop the raisins into small pieces.

4/ Once the ice cream has churned, add the chopped raisins and reserved soaking liquid and mix again. Transfer the ice cream to a plastic container and put into the freezer for 3 hours to harden. Line a tray with baker paper or plastic wrap and place in the freezer to cool down.

5/ Using an ice cream scoop or a spoon, scoop a ball of ice cream onto one of the cookies. Place another cookie on top, then squish them gently together to make an ice cream sandwich. Repeat to make ten equal-sized ice cream sandwiches.

6/ Place the sandwiches on the chilled tray and drizzle each one with the melted chocolate. Return to the freezer to harden for at least 30 minutes before serving on a platter.

Mango tarte tatin.

This is great for either a hot or cold Christmas Day. Here in Oz I cook it outside on the barbecue and then finish it off in the oven. I love making this using the amazing mangoes we get here in summer, but if you are celebrating Chrissy in colder weather, then use seasonal fruit, such as apples or pears, and cook it on the stovetop for an oven finish.

Christmas timeline
If you're under the pump with mains, you could prep the tatin, cook it on the stovetop and then pop it in the oven early on in the day. Leave to cool in the tin and set aside at room temperature then, when you're ready, flash it in the oven for that fresh-cooked effect.

Serves
4–6

Prep time
15 minutes

Cook time
45 minutes

1 sheet good-quality puff pastry
140 g (5 oz) unsalted butter,
    at room temperature
200 g (7 oz) caster (superfine)
    sugar
1 vanilla bean
2 large mangoes, flesh thickly
    sliced
ice cream, whipped cream or
    Custard (page 6), to serve

1/ Preheat the oven to 180°C (350°F). You will need a 20 cm (8 in) diameter ovenproof cast-iron frying pan or tarte tatin tin. Roll out the puff pastry on a lightly floured work surface to a 3 mm (⅛ in) thickness, then cut into a 24 cm (9½ in) disc.

2/ Press the butter into the base of the pan or tin, then sprinkle the sugar evenly over the butter. Split the vanilla bean in half lengthways and scrape out the seeds onto the sugar. Cross the vanilla bean halves over the butter and sugar. Arrange the mango slices over the top, then place the pastry over the fruit, tucking it down the side of the pan and underneath the fruit.

3/ Place the pan on a hot barbecue or stovetop over medium heat. Cook, shaking the pan continuously to avoid it sticking, until syrup starts to form. Use a spoon to baste the entire surface of the pastry with the syrup that bubbles up; this will make the pastry crisp up once it's in the oven. Continue to cook and baste the pastry for about 12 minutes, or until the syrup starts to turn a light amber colour. Remove the pan from the heat and transfer it to the oven. Bake for 25 minutes, or until the pastry is golden brown and crisp.

4/ Leave the tarte tatin to cool for 5 minutes before inverting it onto a piece of baking paper on a plate. Allow to cool slightly, then slide it off onto a serving plate. Coconut ice cream is my favourite with this, but serve it with whatever you fancy.

**WATERMELON +
STRAWBERRY FROSÉ**
P16

**MOSCATO +
RASPBERRY JELLY**
P105

FRUIT SALAD W PEACH SCHNAPPS +
CHAMPAGNE SABAYON
P126

TRISH'S
SHORTBREAD
P136

Fruit salad w̲ peach schnapps ± Champagne sabayon.

You just can't beat fresh fruit at Christmas, and here in Australia where we are at the start of another hot summer, amazing produce is in plentiful supply. Of course you can make fruit salad with any fruits you like, or whatever you have available, so get creative: use exotic combos or keep it simple with just a couple of key fruits. I always prepare fresh fruit for any dinner party, as it is the perfect finish and a great balance to some of the other menu choices. Below are some of my favourites.

Market
Visit your local market and buy what's ripe and in season. You are much better off buying two or three perfectly ripe fruits rather than a huge selection of unripe fruit.

Christmas timeline
Cut the fruit ahead of time if you wish, but not too early – I like to cut the fruit just before serving so it stays fresh and doesn't start to brown. The sabayon will only last for an hour tops before it starts to collapse, so make it fresh after you have cleared mains; it will only take a few minutes anyway.

Prep time
30 minutes

Cook time
Nil

A selection of fruit such as:
pineapple
peach
nectarine
cherries
star fruit
raspberries
strawberries
mango
custard apple
passionfruit
blueberries
watermelon
banana
apricot
oranges
mangosteen
dragon fruit
fig

peach schnapps, to serve
1 lime
Champagne sabayon (page 6),
   to serve

1/ Peel and cut your fruit as you wish and arrange in a bowl. Liberally splash peach schnapps and finely grate lime zest over the fruit. Cover the fruit and leave at room temperature for 20 minutes. Serve with a bowl of Champagne sabayon on the side.

Oat biscuits.

Crumbly and toasty, these oat biscuits are the perfect accompaniment for a Christmas cheeseboard. They go great with all cheeses, but especially cheddars and stilton.

Makes
32

Prep time
20 minutes (plus 1 hour refrigeration)

Cook time
20 minutes

600 g (1 lb 5 oz/4 cups) plain (all-purpose) flour
30 g (1 oz) cream of tartar
40 g (1½ oz) bicarbonate of soda (baking soda)
100 g (3½ oz) caster (superfine) sugar
350 g (12½ oz/3½ cups) rolled (porridge) oats

500 g (1 lb 2 oz) unsalted butter, chilled and diced
6 egg yolks
2 tablespoons milk
salt flakes

1/ Sieve the flour, cream of tartar and bicarbonate of soda into a bowl. Add the sugar and oats. Add the butter, using your fingertips to rub the butter into the flour mixture to form a sandy texture. Add four of the egg yolks and work the mixture with your fingertips to form a dough.

2/ Divide the dough into two equal pieces. Use your hands to roll each piece of dough into a long, even-sized sausage shape. Cover the logs in plastic wrap and refrigerate for 1 hour.

3/ Preheat the oven to 165°C (330°F). Line a baking tray with baking paper. Make an egg wash by mixing the two remaining egg yolks with the milk.

4/ Use a knife to cut the log into 5 mm (¼ in) thick biscuits. Cut sixteen biscuits from each log and lay them on the tray (you can freeze any uncooked dough for later if you like). Lightly brush the biscuits with egg wash and sprinkle with some salt. Bake for 18–20 minutes until golden brown. Remove from the oven and leave to cool on a wire rack.

Garlic ± rosemary–baked Vacherin Mont d'Or.

Irresistible! Wave this in front of the 'I'm too full' crowd after lunch and we'll see who gives in first.

Market
Any small washed-rind soft cheese is perfect for this recipe. Ask your cheesemonger for their recommendations, but preferably you'll need to find a cheese that comes in a wooden case.

Christmas timeline
Prepare the cheese and then leave it in the fridge for up to 2–3 days before serving. Remove and let it come to room temperature for at least 1 hour before baking. You can also roast the garlic the day before.

Serves
4–6

Prep time
15 minutes (plus 30 minutes cooling)

Cook time
55 minutes

1 garlic bulb
1 Vacherin Mont d'Or,
* camembert or similar*
4 small rosemary sprigs
Lavosh (page 22), to serve

1/ Preheat the oven to 180°C (350°F). Wrap the whole garlic bulb in a piece of aluminum foil and place on the oven rack. Roast for 30–45 minutes, then turn the oven off and leave the garlic in the oven to cool for 30 minutes. Remove and set aside.

2/ Preheat the oven again to 180°C (350°F). Remove the cheese from its wooden case and set it aside. Line the case with baking paper, put a sprig of rosemary in the base and then put the cheese back in its case.

3/ Place the cheese in its case on a baking tray. Use a paring knife to make six evenly spaced incisions into the cheese. Pull the roasted garlic bulb apart and separate out the cloves. Stuff each of the six holes alternately with a roasted garlic clove and a sprig of rosemary (use the leftover roasted garlic for flavouring mayonnaises and vinaigrettes). Bake for 8–10 minutes until the cheese feels soft to touch, then remove and serve immediately with pieces of lavosh.

The cheeseboard.

Christmas is not Christmas without overindulging in one of life's greatest pleasures: cheese! Once the pressies are done, and you have one of your grateful relatives stacking the dishwasher for you, then it's time to finish them all off with the cheeseboard.

A cheeseboard can contain as many or as few cheeses as you wish, and the accompaniments again are up to you. They range from a various selection of crackers and lavosh, to cheese biscuits, chutneys, fresh fruit and fruit jellies or pastes. Whatever takes your fancy really, but I would use the following guidelines for a successful and balanced cheeseboard.

Cheese

Try to choose between five and eight cheeses of differing styles. I tend to go for a mix of soft and hard, one or two blues and perhaps a goat's cheese. Some of the world famous cheeses should always be present, but I always try to include something local as well. All cheeses should be at room temperature, so get them out well before you plan to present them. You can make up your cheeseboard and leave it wrapped with a tea towel in the pantry to save time later on.

My ideal Christmas cheeseboard.

Pyengana Clothbound Cheddar
Pyengana, Tasmania

As good as anything you'll find in Europe, this world-class cheddar is, in fact, Australia's oldest farmhouse clothbound cheddar. Pyengana is usually released to the market at 12 months old and has gentle buttery notes and hints of bite. It's a cheese that's perfect for all-day grazing.

Comté
Franche-Comté, France

The second hard cheese is the ever-popular comté, which can be eaten anytime of the day. It exhibits a beautiful floral aroma, with distinct flavours reminiscent of cashews and honey.

Taleggio
Lombardy, Italy

Soft cheese comes in the form of an irresistible taleggio from Italy. This washed-rind cheese has a sweet milky flavour, and a fragrance that has underlying notes of yeast. Only purchase this if it is ripe.

Époisses
France

Pungent, heady and entirely delicious, this soft, washed-rind cheese will perk them up from their afternoon slumber.

Roquefort
Roquefort-sur-Soulzon, France

This raw sheep's milk blue, with its incredibly strong blue notes, is an amazing cheese. It has a fragile melt-in-the-mouth texture and lingering blue spice. It is beautiful when contrasted with fruit spreads, especially plum or cherry. This is also, surprisingly, a pleasant companion to bitter dark chocolate.

Stilton
England

Probably the cheese that has the greatest association with Christmas, this is milder than Roquefort with a slightly courser texture. It is absolutely delicious with walnut bread and is a must in my house at this time of year.

Holy Goat La Luna
Victoria, Australia

A world-class goat cheese from Victoria, Australia, made into a ring shape. These cheese makers produce wonders with goat's milk. They produce many excellent goat cheese products, but this aromatic and creamy cheese is their most famous.

ACCOMPANIMENTS

Cheese straws (page 20)

Olive oil croutons (page 21)

Parmesan grissini (page 21)

Lavosh (page 22)

Oat biscuits (page 127)

muscatels

apples

figs

apricots

pears

grapes

apple jelly

quince paste

cornichons

honey

Sweet treats
± gifts.

(THAT SPECIAL LITTLE SOMETHING)

Cherries in vanilla syrup.

This is such a beautiful gift for friends and family, and it's also a handy component in desserts such as your triumphant Christmas trifle (page 99), in crumbles or simply served on its own with vanilla ice cream. It's worthwhile investing in a cherry pitter to make this job a quick one.

Market
Pectin is a natural gelling agent used to help thicken jams made with fruits that are low in natural pectin. You can buy pectin from supermarkets, health food stores, specialised food ingredient stores or online. It's natural, vegan and gluten free.

Christmas timeline
Cherry season in Oz is around Christmastime, so you can make these a couple of weeks into December. July in Europe, and May to August in the USA, are the best times for cherries. Stored correctly in sterilised jars in the pantry, these cherries will last until Christmas.

Makes
8 x 200 g (7 oz) jars

Prep time
30 minutes

Cook time
10 minutes

30 g (1 oz) pectin
500 g (1 lb 2 oz) caster
*   (superfine) sugar*
500 ml (17 fl oz/2 cups) water
2 vanilla beans, seeds scraped
about 2.5 kg (5½ lb) fresh
*   cherries, pitted (you need*
*   2 kg/4 lb 6 oz pitted cherries)*
juice of 1 lemon

1/ Mix the pectin with the sugar and add this to a large saucepan with the water and vanilla seeds. Whisk to combine well.

2/ Place the pan over medium heat and bring the syrup to the boil, whisking constantly. Reduce the heat to low and simmer for 2 minutes, or until the syrup starts to thicken.

3/ Add the pitted cherries and stir gently until the syrup comes to the boil again, then turn off the heat. Stir in the lemon juice. Leave to cool for 5 minutes, then transfer the cherries and syrup into sterilised jars and seal. Store in the pantry for up to 6 months. Refrigerate after opening and use within a week.

Trish's shortbread.

My mother-in-law, Trish, is the shortbread expert in our family, so I have stolen her recipe. She makes these delicious biscuits every year at Christmas and gives them to us all in beautifully wrapped jars.

Christmas timeline
Get these made in November, so it's not a slog in December, when you've got so many other things to think about. You could make these earlier than November, as they will last up to 6 months once baked.

Makes
**9 shortbread rounds
(4 pieces in each)**

Prep time
20 minutes (plus chilling)

Cook time
45 minutes–1 hour

115 g (4 oz) caster (superfine) sugar
230 g (8 oz) unsalted butter, at room temperature
1 vanilla bean, seeds scraped
315 g (11 oz) plain (all-purpose) flour
60 g (2 oz) cornflour (cornstarch)
canola oil spray

1/ Put the sugar in a food processor and process until finer.

2/ Put the butter in the bowl of a freestanding electric mixer fitted with the paddle attachment. Add the vanilla seeds and cream the butter on low speed until very soft and pale, then increase the speed and add the sugar. Mix to combine well. Sieve the flour and cornflour together, then add to the creamed butter. Turn the machine on low and mix just until a dough forms.

3/ Turn out onto a lightly floured work surface and bring the dough together with your fingers. Divide the dough into nine portions and shape into balls. On a lightly floured work surface, use your hand to pat out the dough balls into 3 cm (1¼ in) thick rounds. Cut into quarters and mark each quarter with a fork.

4/ Preheat the oven to 140°C (275°F). Lightly grease two baking trays with oil spray and line the trays with baking paper. Use your hand to smooth and flatten the paper on the trays.

5/ Place the shortbread pieces on a tray, leaving room between them to allow for expansion. Bake for about 1 hour, checking if they are ready after 45–50 minutes. To know if your shortbread is perfectly cooked, gently lift it up one piece and check the bottom – it should be light golden brown in colour. Remove from the oven, leave to cool a little on the tray before transferring to a wire rack. Once cool, pack the shortbread pieces into biscuit tins or jars tied with ribbon.

Santa's chocolate chip cookies.

This is THE best chocolate chip cookie you'll ever have. Period. Leave these bad boys out on Chrissy Eve for the man in red and you'll jump straight to the nice list.

Christmas timeline
Get a head start by making the recipe up to the dough stage, then roll portions into balls, place on a tray and refrigerate for up to 1 week. Alternatively, the dough balls can be frozen at this stage.

Makes
20 cookies or 1.5 kg (3 lb 5 oz) dough

Prep time
30 minutes (plus chilling)

Cook time
16 minutes (for each batch)

220 g (8 oz) unsalted butter, at room temperature, cubed
200 g (7 oz) soft light brown sugar
180 g (6½ oz) caster (superfine) sugar
20 g (¾ oz) salt
1 teaspoon bicarbonate soda, sieved
1 vanilla bean, seeds scraped
2 eggs
400 g (14 oz/2⅓ cups) plain (all-purpose) flour, sieved
30 g (1 oz) cocoa nibs (see Market, page 146)
200 g (7 oz) melts (buttons) or chopped milk chocolate
300 g (10½ oz) melts (buttons) or chopped dark chocolate

1/ Put the butter, both sugars, salt, bicarbonate of soda and vanilla seeds in the bowl of a freestanding electric mixer fitted with the paddle attachment. Cream on low speed for 8–10 minutes until pale and smooth, using a spatula to scrape down the inside of the bowl to ensure everything is evenly mixed.

2/ Add the eggs, one at a time, beating well and again scraping down the inside of the bowl with the spatula. Add the flour, cocoa nibs, 150 g (5½ oz) of the milk chocolate and 250 g (9 oz) of the dark chocolate (reserving 50 g/1¾ oz each of the milk and dark chocolates for decoration). Beat on low speed until incorporated.

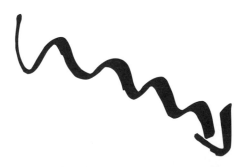

3/ Remove the dough from the machine. Use lightly floured hands and kitchen scales to weigh out 75 g (2¾ oz) portions of dough. Roll the dough portions into balls, place on a tray and refrigerate for a minimum of 30 minutes and up to 1 week (or they can be frozen at this stage).

4/ Preheat the oven to 180°C (350°F). Line a baking tray with baking paper. Transfer the chilled cookie balls onto the prepared tray – I suggest cooking six to eight cookies at a time depending on the size of your oven or tray.

5/ Bake for 16 minutes, then remove the tray from the oven and gently press each cookie down with a weight, such as the base of a saucepan. Do not squash them completely, just flatten them a little. This will make the cookie crunchy on the outside and chewy in the middle.

6/ Dot the reserved melts (buttons) or chopped chocolate onto the surface of the warm cookies. Return the tray to the oven for 30 seconds to melt. Cool on wire racks.

Chocolate brownie.

A good all-rounder, this delicious and super versatile brownie is great on its own served dusted with cocoa, or used as a base for lots of things including the Christmas trifle (page 99) and Rum yum balls (page 146).

Chef's note
If making the brownies for the trifle, double the recipe to make two sponges, and cut out an 18 cm (7 in) diameter disc from each sponge. Use the discs for the trifle and the trimmings for the rum balls.

Makes
One 30 cm x 20 cm (12 in x 8 in) sponge or 24 small squares

Prep time
20 minutes

Cook time
20 minutes

canola oil spray
240 g (8½ oz) unsalted butter, at room temperature, cubed
290 g (10 oz) soft light brown sugar
pinch of salt
140 g (5 oz) dark chocolate, melted (see page 98)
4 eggs
115 g (4 oz/¾ cup) plain (all-purpose) flour
20 g (¾ oz) unsweetened cocoa powder, plus extra for dusting

1/ Preheat the oven to 180°C (350°F) and grease a 2 cm (¾ in) deep, 30 cm x 20 cm (12 in x 8 in) baking tin. Line the base with baking paper and lightly spray the paper with oil spray.

2/ Put the butter, sugar and salt in the bowl of a freestanding electric mixer fitted with the paddle attachment. Cream on medium speed for about 10 minutes until pale and smooth, using a spatula to scrape down the inside of the bowl to ensure everything is evenly mixed.

3/ Add the melted chocolate followed by the eggs, adding them one at a time and mixing until incorporated. Sieve the flour and cocoa powder together and fold into the mixture. Spread the mixture into the tin and level with a palette knife.

4/ Bake for 20 minutes, or until just firm to the touch. Leave to cool in the tin for 15 minutes, then run a knife around the edge of the brownie to loosen it before turning it out onto a wire rack to cool. Cut into 5 cm (2 in) squares and dust with cocoa powder or use as a base for other recipes.

White Christmas cookies.

A thoughtful gift, a fancy place setting or just delicious snacks for the crew at Christmas. These moreish cookies aren't just for the festive season – you'll be busting out trays of these all year round.

Christmas timeline
Make these cookies ahead of time, to free up the mad few days before Christmas for other things. Store for up to 1 month in airtight bags or a container in the pantry.

Makes
About 80 or 10 bags of 8 biscuits

Prep time
30 minutes (plus 1 hour chilling)

Cook time
14 minutes (for each batch)

400 g (14 oz) unsalted butter, at room temperature, cubed
200 g (7 oz) icing (confectioners') sugar
90 g (3 oz/¾ cup) cornflour (cornstarch)
400 g (14 oz/2⅔ cups) plain (all-purpose) flour
50 g (1¾ oz/½ cup) desiccated coconut
200 g (7 oz) dried cranberries, chopped
100 g (3½ oz/⅔ cup) unsalted pistachio nuts, chopped
400 g (14 oz) white chocolate, chopped

1/ Put the butter and icing sugar in the bowl of a freestanding electric mixer fitted with the paddle attachment. Cream on low speed for 8–10 minutes until pale and smooth, using a spatula to scrape down the inside of the bowl to ensure everything is evenly mixed.

2/ Add all of the remaining ingredients, except 300 g (10½ oz) of the chopped chocolate, to the bowl and mix just until the dough comes together.

3/ Transfer the dough to a lightly floured work surface and knead gently into a ball. Flatten the ball and place it between two large sheets of baking paper. Use a rolling pin to roll the dough to a 1 cm (½ in) thickness, then refrigerate for 1 hour.

4/ Preheat the oven to 165°C (330°F). Grease and line two baking trays with baking paper. Using a 4 cm (1½ in) round cutter, cut out cookies from the chilled dough and place them onto the prepared trays, evenly spaced apart. Reroll the scraps and cut out more cookies, to get about eighty in total.

5/ Bake the cookies, one tray at a time, for 14 minutes until light golden. Remove from the oven and leave to cool on the tray. Repeat with the second tray and leave both batches of cookies to cool. Stack all of the cookies onto one tray.

6/ Put the remaining 300 g (10½ oz) chocolate in a plastic bowl and temper it in the microwave (see page 98). Take a cookie and dip it halfway in the chocolate, tap off the excess chocolate and place the half-dipped biscuit onto a tray lined with baking paper. Dip all of the cookies and then leave them to set at room temperature for 30 minutes. If they are still a little tacky, put them in the fridge for 5 minutes to harden.

7/ Divide the biscuits into small cellophane gift bags. Tie with ribbon and a gift tag, to either give as gifts or use a place setting at the Christmas table.

Gingerbread shapes.

Make the dough and get the kids to cut out assorted Christmas shapes, then let them go nuts with frostings and decorations. For something a bit smarter, cut out shapes and use a small plain icing tip to make a small hole at the top. Once baked, thread string or ribbon through the holes and hang as decorations on the tree.

Makes
1.1 kg (2 lb 7 oz) dough

Prep time
30 minutes (plus chilling)

Cook time
12 minutes (for each batch)

250 g (9 oz) honey
35 g (1¼ oz) unsalted butter, at room temperature
550 g (1 lb 3 oz) plain (all-purpose) flour, plus extra for dusting
20 g (¾ oz) gingerbread spice (see Market, page 106)
155 g (5½ oz) caster (superfine) sugar

80 ml (2½ fl oz/⅓ cup) warm water
2 teaspoons bicarbonate of soda (baking soda)
Royal icing (page 145) or melted chocolate (see page 98) for decorating

1/ Put the honey and butter in the bowl of a freestanding electric mixer fitted with the paddle attachment. Beat the ingredients together on low–medium speed until pale and smooth.

2/ Sieve the flour and spice into a bowl. Add the flour and sugar to the honey mix and beat slowly to incorporate. Whisk together the warm water and bicarbonate soda and add to the bowl.

3/ Bring all the ingredients together to form a dough. Remove from the bowl, cover with plastic wrap and transfer to the fridge to rest for 20 minutes.

4/ Preheat the oven to 165°C (330°F) and line a baking tray with baking paper.

5/ Lightly dust the work surface with flour, then use a rolling pin to roll out the dough to a 1 cm (½ in) thickness. Use Christmas cutters to cut out shapes from the gingerbread. Place the biscuits on the tray and bake for 12 minutes. Remove and cool on wire racks before decorating with royal icing or dipping in chocolate. Use as gifts, sweet snacks, tree decorations and gingerbread houses.

Royal icing.

**Makes
about 600 g (1 lb 5 oz)**

*2 egg whites
550 g (1 lb 3 oz/4⅓ cups) icing
    (confectioners') sugar, sieved
1 teaspoon lemon juice
water-soluble food colouring,
    essential oils or freeze-dried
    fruit powders (optional)*

1/ Put the egg whites in a bowl, add half the sieved icing sugar and mix with a whisk. Add the remaining icing sugar 1 tablespoon at a time, until you have a thick, smooth consistency that will not spread when piped. Because egg white sizes can vary, you may need more or less icing sugar than the amount specified.

2/ Mix in the lemon juice. If you like, add your preferred colourings or flavourings at this stage. Transfer to a piping (icing) bag and use to decorate the gingerbread, or biscuits and cakes.

Rum yum balls.

Super simple and delicious, these rums balls are made with leftover sponge – I make them with the brownie scraps from the Christmas trifle (page 99). They're called rum balls, but you can use any alcoholic spirit to give these some festive cheer.

Market
Cocoa nibs will add an earthy cocoa crunch and can be bought from health food stores or speciality ingredient suppliers. Gold lustre powder is an edible food decoration and can be bought from speciality ingredient suppliers.

Makes
30

Prep time
20 minutes (plus chilling)

Cook time
Nil

300 g (10½ oz) Chocolate brownie scraps (page 140), frozen
100 g (3½ oz) Santa's chocolate chip cookies (page 137), crumbled, or use any cookie you like
100 g (3½ oz) milk chocolate, finely chopped
50 g (1¾ oz) cocoa nibs
1 tablespoon unsweetened cocoa powder
3 tablespoons dark rum
300 g (10½ oz) dark chocolate, tempered (see page 98)
gold lustre powder for dusting

1/ Line two trays with baking paper and set aside. Put the frozen chocolate brownie scraps into a blender and quickly pulse to form crumbs. If you do this for too long, the sponge will defrost and go mushy.

2/ Pour the cold blitzed crumbs into a bowl with the cookie crumbs, milk chocolate, cocoa nibs, cocoa powder and rum. Mix the contents of the bowl with your fingertips and then form the mixture into bite-sized balls. Squash the balls to compact them, then place on one of the prepared trays – you should have about thirty balls. Refrigerate for 20 minutes to firm up.

3/ Leave the tempered chocolate in the bowl, stirring occasionally until it is in a soft, semi-solid state. Then scoop up a small quantity of chocolate with your hand and roll it around a cold rum ball. Place the chocolate-covered ball on the remaining clean tray and then repeat this step until all the balls are covered in chocolate. Refrigerate for 10 minutes to harden. Remove from the fridge and brush gold powder over the rum balls.

Strawberry ± mint white chocolate rubble.

This is one of the biggest selling products in my Sweet Studio in Melbourne. It is popular all year round even though the freeze-dried red strawberries and green mint make it look especially Christmassy.

Market

I use a company called Fresh As for my freeze-dried ingredients. Alternatively look online or go to a specialist food ingredient supplier; you might also find them in some health food stores and supermarkets. The freeze-dried or chopped mint isn't essential here, as most of the mint flavour in this rubble comes from the mint oil, but it does make the end product look more attractive. You'll find mint oil in health food stores or online. Make sure it is a food safe additive.

Makes

400 g (14 oz) or 4 x 100 g (3½ oz) bags for gifts

Prep time

15 minutes (plus setting)

Cook time

Nil

canola oil spray
½ teaspoon mint oil
400 g (14 oz) white chocolate, tempered (see page 98)
30 g (1 oz) freeze-dried strawberry slices
5 g (¼ oz) freeze-dried or chopped dried mint leaves (optional)

1/ Lightly spray a 3 cm (1¼ in) deep, 35 cm x 25 cm (14 in x 10 in) baking tray with oil spray and line the base with a piece of baking paper.

2/ Mix the mint oil into the tempered chocolate and pour most of the chocolate into the tray to cover the base. Randomly stud the chocolate with the strawberry slices and mint leaves, if using. Gently tap the tray on the table a couple of times to level. Flick the remaining chocolate over the top using a spoon, and again tap to flatten.

3/ Leave the tray to set at cool room temperature for 30 minutes. To speed things up, place in the fridge for 15 minutes.

4/ Break into irregular pieces and store in between pieces of baking paper in a tin or sealed container. The chocolate pieces can also be packed into cellophane bags for a beautiful Christmas present or stocking filler.

Christmas hedgehog.

What is a hedgehog? And, what do these prickly little fellas have to do with Christmas? Well, it's a classic Aussie chocolate-based biscuit slice, it's delicious, and it's perfect to have on standby for when unexpected guests drop in – or whip one up to give to someone as a thoughtful gift. It's great with tea or coffee during the day or as an after dinner sweet treat, and – the best part – it's dead easy to make.

Market
Gianduja is a mix of sweetened chocolate and hazelnut paste; it comes in a block and can be melted and used like chocolate. Buy it from specialist ingredient stores. Cocoa nibs will add an earthly cocoa crunch and can be bought from health food or specialist ingredient stores.

Christmas timeline
This can be made well in advance of the hectic period – even a couple of weeks beforehand, as it will store well in a sealed container in the pantry. Just don't be tempted to nibble on it, because once you start, you won't be able to stop!

Makes
About 60 small pieces

Prep time
25 minutes (plus setting)

Cook time
Nil

canola oil spray
400 g (14 oz) Santa's chocolate
    chip cookies (page 137)
100 g (3½ oz) flaked almonds,
    lightly toasted
60 g (2 oz) pistachio nuts,
    roughly chopped
40 g (1½ oz) cocoa nibs
50 g (1¾ oz) dried cranberries,
    chopped
400 g (14 oz) gianduja, melted
    (see page 98)
400 g (14 oz) dark chocolate,
    melted (see page 98)
pinch of salt

1/ Lightly spray a 2 cm (¾ in) deep, 30 cm x 20 cm (12 in x 8 in) baking tin with oil spray. Cut a piece of baking paper to the exact width of the base of the tray, but longer by 10 cm (4 in). Line the tray with the paper and use your hand to smooth and flatten the paper on the tray.

2/ Chop the chocolate chip cookies into small pieces, around 2 cm (¾ in) in length. Put the chopped chocolate in a bowl and add the almonds, pistachios, cocoa nibs and dried cranberries.

3/ Combine the melted gianduja and melted chocolate in a bowl, add the salt and mix well. Pour this onto the dry ingredients and stir to combine well, then pour into the prepared tray, ensuring the mixture is pressed into the sides of the tray. Don't press down or smooth the mixture – you want to keep the surface uneven. Gently tap the tray on the table to eliminate any air bubbles. Refrigerate the hedgehog for 15 minutes to set.

4/ Run a small paring knife around the edge of the hedgehog to loosen it from the tin, then use the overhanging paper flaps to lift it out of the tin and onto a chopping board. Cut into 2 cm (¾ in) thick slices, then cut these slices into smaller pieces. Transfer to a serving plate.

CHRISTMAS
HEDGEHOG
p149

STRAWBERRY + MINT
WHITE CHOCOLATE
RUBBLE
p148

Coffee-infused rum ± dark chocolate truffles.

A decadent ending to a decadent celebration lunch, these will keep them going until cheese on toast later in the evening, especially with that extra little buzz from the coffee.

Christmas timeline
Make these a couple of weeks before serving and store in the fridge until needed. Serve them with coffee after lunch, or pack into small bags to give as gifts.

Makes
40

Prep time
30 minutes (plus overnight infusion and cooling time)

Cook time
30 minutes

20 g (¾ oz) coffee beans
320 ml (11 fl oz) thickened (whipping) cream
1 tablespoon honey
canola oil spray
475 g (1 lb 1 oz) chopped dark chocolate (67% cocoa solids), or melts (buttons)
pinch of salt
2 tablespoons rum
20 g (¾ oz) unsalted butter
200 g (7 oz) unsweetened cocoa powder

1/ Preheat the oven to 120°C (250°F). Line a baking tray with baking paper. Place the coffee beans on the tray and warm them in the oven for 20 minutes.

2/ Put the cream and honey in a saucepan and bring to the boil. Remove from the heat and add the lightly roasted coffee beans. Leave to cool for 20 minutes before covering the pan with plastic wrap and placing it in the fridge to infuse overnight.

3/ Lightly spray a flat tray with oil spray and line with baking paper. Use your hand to smooth and flatten the paper on the tray.

4/ The next day, put the chocolate in a tall narrow plastic container, such as a jug. Remove the saucepan from the fridge and place over medium heat. Bring to the boil and then strain the mixture through a sieve onto the chocolate in the jug. Add the salt, rum and butter and leave to sit for 30 seconds. Blend with a hand-held stick blender until the ganache is smooth and shiny. Lay plastic wrap over the surface of the ganache and leave it to harden at room temperature for around 3 hours.

5/ Transfer the ganache to a piping (icing) bag fitted with a 2 cm (¾ in) plain tip and pipe small bulbs onto the prepared tray. Place the tray in the fridge for 10 minutes to harden slightly.

6/ Tip the cocoa powder into a shallow tray or container. Working with a few bulbs of ganache at a time, roll them into irregular-shaped spheres and then drop them in the cocoa powder, rolling them around to coat. Once all of the truffles have been coated, store them in the fridge.

Salted caramels.

There should be a public holiday for salted caramel!

Makes
100 small caramels

Prep time
15 minutes (plus overnight setting)

Cook time
20 minutes

canola oil spray
800 ml (27 fl oz) thickened (whipping) cream
1 vanilla bean, seeds scraped
420 g (15 oz) caster (superfine) sugar
140 g (5 oz) glucose
325 g (11½ oz) unsalted butter, at room temperature

60 g (2 oz) honey
10 g (¼ oz) salt
½ teaspoon bicarbonate of soda (baking soda)
salt flakes, to finish

1/ Lightly spray a 30 cm (12 in) square non-stick shallow baking tin with canola spray.

2/ Put the cream and vanilla seeds in a saucepan and bring to the boil. Turn off the heat and leave the pan on the side of the stove.

3/ Pour the sugar, bit by bit, into a large saucepan over medium heat, stirring constantly with a wooden spoon until the sugar melts and starts to form a caramel. Continue cooking and stirring until all of the sugar has dissolved and the caramel is a deep amber colour.

4/ Deglaze the pan with the reserved warm cream. Take care when you add the cream, as the caramel will splatter and expand furiously. Whisk and then add the glucose, butter, honey and salt. Cook, whisking constantly, until you reach 118°C (244°F); use a digital or sugar thermometer to accurately check the temperature.

5/ Turn off the heat, add the bicarbonate of soda and mix well. Pour this mix evenly into the tin, scraping all the caramel out of the pan. Gently tap the tin to burst any bubbles and level. Cover the tray with plastic wrap and leave to set overnight at room temperature.

6/ The next day, run a small paring knife around the edges of the caramel to loosen it. Invert the tin onto a chopping board and use the tip of the knife to pull the caramel down and out of the tin.

7/ Use an oiled cook's knife to cut the caramel into 2 cm x 3 cm (¾ in x 1¼ in) pieces. Lightly sprinkle some salt flakes over the top of each piece. Roll the salted caramels in clear plastic sweet wrappers or small squares of baking paper and pop them in gift bags. Alternatively, serve them unwrapped on a dish or tray for a sweet treat after lunch or dinner.

Soft-set pineapple jam <u>w</u> lime, vanilla ± star anise.

Homemade gifts are the best gifts, and this little jar of sweet sunshine will be well received by everyone. If they ask what they can do with it, tell them to drizzle it over ice cream or use it to spread inside a sponge. But what you'll be doing with yours is glazing your ham (see page 83) like a champion for real Christmas wow factor!

Market
Don't be tempted to use tinned pineapples please, as you'll be able to tell the difference. Use fresh, remembering that once pineapples are picked they don't ripen further, so you'll have to pick out good ones: it should smell fresh, not fermented; feel firm but not too hard if squeezed; and feel heavy for its size.

Christmas timeline
Pineapples are pretty much available all year round, so get ahead by making this one in October or November.

Makes
8 x 275 g (9½ oz) jars

Prep time
15 minutes

Cook time
30 minutes

1.5 kg (3 lb 5 oz) pineapple flesh
35 g (1¼ oz) pectin (see Market, page 134)
1.5 kg (3 lb 5 oz) caster (superfine) sugar
2 vanilla beans, seeds scraped
finely grated zest and juice of 4 limes
16 star anise

1/ Put the pineapple flesh in a blender and whiz until coarsely puréed. Mix the pectin with the sugar and add this to a large heavy-based saucepan with the puréed pineapple and vanilla seeds. Stir to combine well.

2/ Place the pan over medium heat and bring to the boil, stirring constantly with a spatula to ensure it does not catch on the base of the pan. Cook the jam to 103°C (217°F); use a sugar or digital thermometer to accurately check the temperature. Be careful, as the jam tends to spit and splatter as the temperature increases.

3/ Once the jam reaches the correct temperature, remove the pan from the heat and add the lime zest and juice. Stir well and leave to cool a little. Put two star anise into each sterilised jar and then ladle or pour the jam into the jars. Store in the pantry for up to 3 months. Refrigerate after opening and use within 1 month.

Raspberry ± whisky jam.

'Tipsy jam' I call this, beautiful in desserts, cakes, slices or on toast! This makes a thoughtful homemade gift for someone at Christmas as well. The whisky can be left out for a just-as-delicious non-alcoholic version.

Christmas timeline
Get this made when raspberries are in season wherever you are. Whenever that is, the jam will last until Christmas if stored in sterilised jars.

Makes
8 x 200 g (7 oz) jars

Prep time
10 minutes

Cook time
15 minutes

10 g (¼ oz) pectin
  (see Market, page 134)
500 g (1 lb 2 oz) caster
  (superfine) sugar
500 g (1 lb 2 oz) fresh or frozen
  raspberries (thawed if frozen)
juice of ½ lemon
glug of whisky

1/ Mix the pectin with the sugar and add this to a heavy-based saucepan with the raspberries. Mash the ingredients together with a fork. Heat the fruit over medium heat, stirring frequently with a wooden spoon or spatula, until it comes to the boil.

2/ Add a sugar or digital thermometer to the pan and continue to cook, stirring regularly. Be careful at this stage, as the jam is very hot and may start to bubble and spit as you stir the pot. Cook the jam to a temperature of 103°C (217°F) and then remove from the heat. Gently stir in the lemon juice and whisky.

3/ Immediately pour into sterilised jars, then pour a small quantity of whisky onto the surface of the jam before putting the lid on. This makes sure there is a heady aroma when the jar is opened. Store in a cool pantry for up to 1 year. If you aren't giving the jam as gifts, pour it into a couple of containers, pour whisky onto the surface, and allow the jam to cool before covering and storing in the fridge for up to 6 months.

Christmas pudding French toast.

'Oh I wish it could be Christmas ev'ry daaaaay,' sang Wizzard. Well it can be, certainly on Boxing Day, at least.

Serves
4

Prep time
15 minutes (plus 2 hours soaking)

Cook time
10 minutes

300 ml (10 fl oz) full-cream (whole) milk
3 eggs
200 g (7 oz) caster (superfine) sugar
3 tablespoons brandy, plus a splash extra to serve
4 slices leftover Christmas pudding (page 114), 2 cm (¾ in) thick
80 g (2¾ oz) unsalted butter
ice cream, to serve

1/ Pour the milk into a bowl and add the eggs, 50 g (1¾ oz) of the sugar and the brandy. Mix well and then strain through a sieve into a jug.

2/ Place the slices of Christmas pudding in a shallow dish and pour over the custard mix. Refrigerate for a minimum of 2 hours. After 1 hour, flip all the slices over to get maximum coverage. Drain the slices on a wire rack set over a tray to catch the drips.

3/ Heat the remaining sugar in a non-stick frying pan over medium heat until just melted and starting to turn golden brown. Reduce the heat to low and add the butter, swirling it around in the pan until fully mixed in.

4/ Add the drained slices of Christmas pudding and cook them for a couple of minutes until brown and caramelised. Flip them over with a spatula and cook for the same amount of time on the other side. Remove from the pan and serve with ice cream and a splash of brandy.

Crab, if you're lucky, omelette.

Urgh! Feeling a bit seedy after yesterday's shenanigans? Well chef, you'd better knock up one of these for yourself before the troops wake up, cos you're on breakfast duty. If you are lucky there's a bit of crab left over. There's never enough for everyone and you're up early, so take advantage of chef rights and take it! This will sort you out.

Serves
1

Prep time
10 minutes

Cook time
5 minutes

50 g (1¾ oz) unsalted butter
3 eggs, lightly beaten with a fork
100 g (3½ oz) crab meat (use
    prawns if you're out of luck)
salt flakes
freshly ground black pepper
1 red bird's eye chilli, seeded
    and chopped
1 tablespoon chopped fresh
    herbs, such as chives,
    parsley or coriander (cilantro)
    leaves, or a mix will do

1 handful rocket (arugula)
1 spring onion (scallion),
    trimmed and thinly sliced
    diagonally

1/ Preheat the grill (broiler) to high.

2/ Heat an 18 cm (7 in) non-stick omelette pan over medium heat for 3 minutes. Add the butter and let it melt, then add the beaten eggs and reduce the heat to low. Cook for 45 seconds, moving the egg around with a fork.

3/ Sprinkle the crab evenly over the top of the wet egg, then season with salt and pepper. Add the chilli and chopped herbs and give it all a stir again with the fork.

4/ Remove the pan from the heat and place under the hot grill on the top shelf for 1 minute to set. Slide the omelette onto a plate and sprinkle with rocket and spring onion.

SNAP SNAP

New Year's Day detox breakfast bowl.

That's it! I'm never eating so much food again, I'm never EVER drinking again and I'm going to lose some weight, starting now!

<u>Serves</u>
1

<u>Prep time</u>
15 minutes (plus overnight freezing)

<u>Cook time</u>
Nil

100 g (3½ oz) raspberries
120 g (4½ oz) strawberries, hulled
60 g (2 oz) blueberries
120 g (4½ oz) cherries, pitted
1 banana, chopped
¼ pomegranate, seeds
20 g (¾ oz) flaked almonds, toasted

1/ Before you go to bed, freeze 80 g (2¾ oz) of the raspberries, 100 g (3½ oz) strawberries, 50 g (1¾ oz) blueberries, 100 g (3½ oz) cherries and the chopped banana.

2/ The next morning, put the frozen fruit into a blender and blend to a thick and smooth frozen smoothie.

3/ Transfer to a bowl and top with the remaining raspberries, strawberries (sliced), blueberries and cherries. Scatter the pomegranate seeds and toasted almonds over the top. Eat and feel righteous.

REMAINS
164

Fried polenta w̲ bacon, tomato ± mushrooms.

Whenever you make soft polenta (see page 44) it's inevitable that you'll make more than you'll need, so spread the leftovers into a shallow tray lined with plastic wrap and refrigerate. The next day, cut the polenta in equal-sized pieces and turn them into a stunning breakfast. Adjust the quantities of the recipe to suit however much polenta you have.

Serves
4

Prep time
10 minutes

Cook time
20 minutes

8 streaky bacon slices
4 tomatoes, cut in half
salt flakes
freshly ground black pepper
100 ml (3½ fl oz) light olive oil
4 polenta pieces, 5 cm (2 in) square
80 g (2¾ oz) parmesan
250 g (9 oz) Swiss brown mushrooms, sliced

90 g (3 oz) unsalted butter
1 tablespoon worcestershire sauce
1 tablespoon chopped fresh thyme
juice from ¼ lemon

1/ Preheat the grill (broiler) to high. Grill (broil) the bacon and tomato halves until the bacon is browned and crispy and the tomatoes are soft. Season the tomatoes with salt and pepper and set aside with the bacon.

2/ Preheat the oven to 160°C (320°F). Line a baking tray with baking paper. Heat half the oil in a non-stick frying pan over medium heat. Add the polenta squares and fry for 3–4 minutes on each side. Transfer the polenta to the tray and grate over the parmesan. Add the bacon and tomatoes to the tray and put in the oven to keep warm. Turn the oven off.

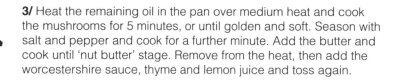

3/ Heat the remaining oil in the pan over medium heat and cook the mushrooms for 5 minutes, or until golden and soft. Season with salt and pepper and cook for a further minute. Add the butter and cook until 'nut butter' stage. Remove from the heat, then add the worcestershire sauce, thyme and lemon juice and toss again.

4/ Remove the tray from the oven and serve the polenta slices with the bacon and tomatoes. Spoon the mushrooms and some pan juices over the polenta.

Tomato, chilli ± prawn spaghetti.

Super quick and delicious – that's what your guests want and what you NEED on Boxing Day.

Serves
4–6

Prep time
15 minutes

Cook time
25 minutes

500 g (1 lb 2 oz) spaghetti
3 tablespoons light olive oil
2 French shallots, finely diced
2 garlic cloves, peeled
2 red bird's eye chillies,
* chopped with seeds*
salt flakes
600 g (1 lb 5 oz) cherry
* tomatoes, halved*
500 g (1 lb 2 oz) cooked, peeled
* prawns (shrimp), chopped*
* into chunks*

finely grated zest of 1 lemon
freshly ground black pepper
2 tablespoons chopped fresh
* flat-leaf (Italian) parsley*
2 tablespoons chopped fresh
* coriander (cilantro) leaves*
100 g (3½ oz) parmesan

1/ Bring a large saucepan of salted water to the boil, add the spaghetti and cook until al dente.

2/ Meanwhile, heat a large cast-iron or heavy-based saucepan over medium heat. Add the oil and shallot, then grate in the garlic using a microplane. Add the chilli and a pinch of salt and cook for a few minutes, stirring constantly, until the onion has softened.

3/ Add the cherry tomatoes and cook for 3 minutes, then add the prawns and lemon zest. Season with salt and pepper and cook for a further 4–5 minutes.

4/ Drain the spaghetti and add it to the sauce along with the herbs. Remove from the heat and stir to coat the spaghetti in the sauce. Grate the parmesan over the top and serve from the pan.

Cheeseboard pasta bake.

Perfect for the day after the night before, this won't take much effort to get onto the table and everyone will thank you for it. Use whatever cheese you like or had left on that epic cheeseboard from last night. Even blue cheese works well in this.

Serves
6

Prep time
15 minutes

Cook time
45 minutes

500 g (1 lb 2 oz) penne
2 tablespoons light olive oil
1 red onion, finely diced
2 garlic cloves, peeled
1 teaspoon fresh thyme
salt flakes
350 ml (12 fl oz) thickened (whipping) cream
500 g (1 lb 2 oz) whatever cheese you have left over from the Christmas cheeseboard

4 tablespoons chopped fresh flat-leaf (Italian) parsley
120 g (4½ oz) sourdough, crusts removed and bread torn into small pieces
finely grated zest of ½ lemon
freshly ground black pepper

1/ Preheat the oven to 180°C (350°F). Bring a large saucepan of salted water to the boil, add the pasta and cook for 2 minutes less than the recommended time on the packet.

2/ Meanwhile, heat a large cast-iron or heavy-based saucepan over medium heat. Add the oil and onion, then grate in the garlic using a microplane. Add the thyme and a pinch of salt and cook for a few minutes, stirring constantly, until the onion has softened.

3/ Drain the pasta, reserving some of the cooking water. Add the pasta to the pan with the onions, stir to mix well, then add a couple of ladles of pasta water and stir. Pour in the cream followed by three-quarters of the cheese and stir to melt the cheese. Stir in three-quarters of the parsley, season with salt and pepper and pour into a baking dish. Level the pasta out and stud the top with the remaining cheese.

4/ Mix the bread pieces in a bowl with the remaining parsley, the lemon zest and some salt and pepper, and scatter over the top of the pasta. Bake for 35 minutes, or until crispy on top and bubbling underneath. Serve with a green salad and vinaigrette.

Christmas movies

While you're getting everything done, you don't need people bothering you in your natural habitat…the kitchen! Not unless you've got some jobs for them like peeling potatoes and washing up. So you need a back-up plan and a Christmas movie is it. Bang one of these on to keep them occupied while you whip up a feast.

I've listed the movies in order of their running times, so you can choose the movie to suit the exact prep time of your dish.

THE SNOWMAN
1982 • 27 m

A CHARLIE BROWN CHRISTMAS
1965 • 30 m

A VERY MURRAY CHRISTMAS
2015 • 56 m

THE NIGHTMARE BEFORE CHRISTMAS
1993 • 1 h 16 m

RARE EXPORTS: A CHRISTMAS TALE
2010 • 1 h 24 m

HAPPY CHRISTMAS
2014 • 1 h 28 m

FOUR CHRISTMASES
2008 • 1 h 28 m

THE MUPPET CHRISTMAS CAROL
1992 • 1 h 29 m

A CHRISTMAS STORY
1983 • 1 h 34 m

SILENT NIGHT
2012 • 1 h 34 m

JINGLE ALL THE WAY
1996 • 1 h 35 m

SANTA'S SLAY
2005 • 1 h 35 m

A CHRISTMAS CAROL
2009 • 1 h 36 m

ELF
2003 • 1 h 37 m

NATIONAL LAMPOON'S CHRISTMAS VACATION
1989 • 1 h 37 m

ARTHUR CHRISTMAS
2011 • 1 h 37 m

THE SANTA CLAUSE
1994 • 1 h 37 m

BLACK CHRISTMAS
1974 • 1 h 38 m

BAD SANTA
2003 • 1 h 38 m

CHRISTMAS WITH THE KRANKS
2004 • 1 h 39 m

POLAR EXPRESS
2004 • 1 h 40 m

HOLIDAY INN
1942 • 1 h 41 m

THE NIGHT BEFORE
2015 • 1 h 41 m

SCROOGED
1988 • 1 h 41 m

CHRISTMAS IN CONNECTICUT
1945 • 1 h 42 m

HOME ALONE
1990 • 1 h 43

THE SANTA CLAUSE 2
2002 • 1 h 45 m

GREMLINS
1984 • 1 h 47 m

SANTA CLAUS: THE MOVIE
1985 • 1 h 48 m

HOW THE GRINCH STOLE CHRISTMAS
2000 • 1 h 50 m

MEET ME IN ST LOUIS
1944 • 1 h 53 m

MIRACLE ON 34TH STREET
1994 • 1 h 54 m

FRED CLAUS
2007 • 1 h 56 m

TRADING PLACES
1983 • 1 h 58 m

HOME ALONE 2: LOST IN NEW YORK
1992 • 2 h 1 m

DIE HARD
1988 • 2 h 12 m

IT'S A WONDERFUL LIFE
1946 • 2 h 12 m

THE HOLIDAY
2006 • 2 h 18 m

WHITE CHRISTMAS
1954 • 2 h 20 m

LOVE ACTUALLY
2003 • 2 h 25 m

Christmas playlist

It's not Christmas without some cheesy songs to get you all in the spirit! I love Christmas and have carefully curated my playlist over many years. I have eliminated some annoying ones and added a few new classics to my list. This list gets played on high while I'm cooking away in the kitchen, either at work or at home. I really can't cook without music and I look forward to this special playlist every year.

Whether 'Do they know it's Christmas?' is your fave or you think 'Careless Whisper' can't be topped, they are all here. Chris Rea, Bruce Springsteen and Mariah Carey all make an appearance, as well as my fave Aussie Christmas classics, such as Paul Kelly 'Making Gravy' and Kylie & Dannii singing '100 degrees'.

Please take time to follow me, Darren Purchese, on Spotify and download or stream the 'Chefs host Christmas too' playlist. Enjoy!

These are the top ten that really get me rocking:

LAST CHRISTMAS
Wham!

ALL I WANT FOR CHRISTMAS IS YOU
Mariah Carey

100 DEGREES
Kylie and Dannii Minogue

HOW TO MAKE GRAVY
Paul Kelly

DO THEY KNOW IT'S CHRISTMAS?
Band Aid

SUNSHINE
Sia

CHRISTMAS IN HOLLIS
RUN-D.M.C.

DRIVING HOME FOR CHRISTMAS
Chris Rea

I DON'T WANT TO FIGHT TONIGHT
The Ramones

WHO TOOK THE MERRY OUT OF CHRISTMAS
The Staple Singers

Finding things.

Thank you.

FOR BEING A FRIEND...

Festive thanks to everyone who helped make it all happen in my marshmallow world.

#teamCHCT
Jane Willson – the best x
Marg Bowman
Ari Hatzis
Caroline Velik
Vaughan Mossop
Kim Rowney

#teamDarrenPurchese
Cath Claringbold
Gary McBean and family – Gary's Quality Meats, Prahran Market
Joe Chahin – BR Wellington
Dempsey Smythe – BR Wellington
Roberta Barichello – Printcess
Claude Barichello – Bertocchi Smallgoods
Christean Ng – Burch & Purchese
Nichole Horvath – Burch & Purchese
Blaze Yiap – Burch & Purchese
David Van Rooy – Vanrooy Machinery
Duncan Black – Vanrooy Machinery
James Stone – Vanrooy Machinery
Filiz Bensan – KitchenAid Australia
'Scuba' Steve Vaughan – MFJ, for getting me fit enough to pull off that Christmas sweater look

Who's Darren?

I think it's pretty obvious here that Darren really does love Christmas! It's the sweetest time of year for him, his wife Cath and the team at his Burch & Purchese Sweet Studio in Melbourne. After the cheesy success of *Chefs Eat Toasties Too*, Darren now turns his hand to making the ultimate Christmas cookbook. Years of working a double shift on Christmas Day and catering for large family occasions make Darren well qualified to help out with the cooking on the biggest day of the year. Darren's trademark sweet tricks are all here, complemented by his savoury triumphs, decadent gifts and some of his most festive drinks and nibbles.

GET SOCIAL

Chefs Host Christmas Too is the second in Darren's *Chefs...Too* series of cookbooks. Stay updated by following us on the social channels below:

Instagram @ChefsEat

Twitter @ChefsEatBooks

Facebook @ChefsEatBooks

Use the #ChefsHostChristmas hashtag when posting pics of your creations using the recipes from this book, and we will share and repost them.

Published in 2018 by Hardie Grant Books,
an imprint of Hardie Grant Publishing

Hardie Grant Books (Melbourne)
Building 1, 658 Church Street
Richmond, Victoria 3121

Hardie Grant Books (London)
5th & 6th Floors
52–54 Southwark Street
London SE1 1UN

hardiegrantbooks.com

A catalogue record for this
book is available from the
National Library of Australia

NATIONAL
LIBRARY
OF AUSTRALIA

Chefs Host Christmas Too
ISBN 978 1 74379 478 4

Publishing Director: Jane Willson
Managing Editor: Marg Bowman
Editor: Kim Rowney
Concept Design: Mark Campbell
Designer: Vaughan Mossop @ NBHD Creative
Photographer: Ari Hatzis
Stylist: Caroline Velik
Indexer: Neil Daly
Design Manager: Jessica Lowe
Production Manager: Todd Rechner

Colour reproduction by Splitting Image Colour Studio
Printed in China by 1010 Printing International Limited

TILL NEXT YEAR